YOU GOTTA HAVE
BALLS

YOU GOTTA HAVE BALLS

How a Kid from Brooklyn Started from Scratch,
Bought Yankee Stadium,
and Created a Sports Empire

BRANDON STEINER

WILEY

John Wiley & Sons, Inc.

Cover image: Anthony Causi
Cover design: Michael J. Freeland

Published by John Wiley & Sons, Inc., Hoboken, New Jersey.
Published simultaneously in Canada.

For general information on our other products and services or for technical support, please contact our Customer Care Department within the United States at (800) 762-2974, outside the United States at (317) 572-3993 or fax (317) 572-4002.

Wiley publishes in a variety of print and electronic formats and by print-on-demand. Some material included with standard print versions of this book may not be included in e-books or in print-on-demand. If this book refers to media such as a CD or DVD that is not included in the version you purchased, you may download this material at http://booksupport.wiley.com. For more information about Wiley products, visit www.wiley.com.

Library of Congress Cataloging-in-Publication Data:

Steiner, Brandon.
  You gotta have balls : how a kid from Brooklyn started from scratch, bought Yankee Stadium, and created a sports empire / Brandon Steiner.
     p. cm.
  Includes index.
   ISBN 978-1-118-17207-0 (hardback); ISBN 978-1-118-33035-7 (ebk); ISBN 978-1-118-33104-0 (ebk); ISBN 978-1-118-33319-8 (ebk)
  1. Sports—New York (State)—New York—Marketing. 2. Sports—Collectibles—New York (State)—New York. I. Title.
  GV585.5.N4S84 2012
  796.0688—dc23

                                                                2012020271

Printed in the United States of America

10 9 8 7 6 5 4 3 2 1

This book is dedicated to the three most important women in my life:

For my mother, Evelyn. Everything I've ever learned can be traced back to something she once taught me. I try to live up to her no-fear attitude and her limitless compassion for people every day. Her favorite saying was: "You gotta have balls."

For my wife, Mara. My most unsung, but biggest hero—I still get butterflies when I see you walk by my office. You are and always will be the love of my life.

And for my daughter, Nicole. I like to count myself an avid collector of people, but even at her age, Nicole brings them together more quickly than I ever have.

CONTENTS

ACKNOWLEDGMENTS

T hank you to my son, Crosby, who will be anything he wants to be and more.

Thank you to our stepson, Keith Martinez, who reminds me that anything is possible. What an amazing story you turned out to be.

Thank you to my brother, Adam, who made the biggest comeback of all time, and has helped more people stop smoking than I imagined possible.

I'm grateful to my fellow Brooklynite and dreamer, Colby Brin. I started this book with countless threads of memories, experiences, and ideas in mind; I wanted to share them with the reader, but I wasn't sure how they fit together. Colby helped me weave them into the narrative that makes up these pages. I couldn't have done it without him.

The same goes for Steve Costello, Eric Levy, A. J. Romero, Andrew Rasero, Chris Amoroso, Brett Schissler, Kelvin Joseph, Sean Mahoney, Margaret Adams, and the entire Steiner Sports family. Thank you for making my dreams come true every day. It's an honor to work with all of you.

And of course all my friends from the Brooklyn schoolyards who have been there from the beginning and I know have my back until the end.

I'll always be grateful to Alzie Jackson, my old camp mentor.

Thanks to Matt Weinberg for always making sure Steiner Sports has had the best transportation.

Thanks to Shannon Vargo, Elana Schulman, Heather Condon, Peter Knox, Linda Indig, and the entire John Wiley & Sons team.

Thanks to my in-house marketing squad: Cassidy Mara, Thomas Hanvey, and Zachary Karow.

I am deeply grateful to the New York Yankees and the entire Yankee family. And the Steinbrenner family.

Special thanks to Randy Levine, for being the original visionary behind Yankees-Steiner, and my biggest fan; and to Randy Weisenburger, for being the Yankees-Steiner *closer*.

Thanks to the Dallas Cowboys; Notre Dame and Notre Dame Football; Madison Square Garden and Jim Dolan; Scott O'Neal; the Syracuse University Athletic Department; my friend Daryl Gross; Michael Veley and David Salanger; David Falk, for bringing me closer to Syracuse and having the vision to build the best sports management school on the planet.

Thanks to my idol Oprah Winfrey, for so much inspiration and so many aha moments. Over the 25 years she aired her show, I didn't miss many episodes. Now she has her own network. Talk about balls.

Thank you to Frank Bisignano, one of the smartest guys I have ever met, who taught me how to adjust when "the circumstances have changed."

Big thanks to Harvey Mackay and the Mackay Roundtable for constant help and mentoring, and for showing me how to put together a book I could be proud of. As we like to say, *None of us is as smart as all of us.*

PROLOGUE

LAST CALL AT YANKEE STADIUM

When I was a kid growing up in Brooklyn, I lived for the summer. Summer brought the gifts of camp and all-day sports, as opposed to the burdens of school and studying. It was in summer that our little apartment on Kings Highway wouldn't be freezing when I woke up in the morning. And maybe most importantly, summer days had the potential to turn into afternoons spent at my favorite place in the world: Yankee Stadium.

My family didn't have season tickets or anything. My father was out of the picture; my mother was often sick, bouncing between the hospital and our house; and my two brothers had their own problems. For God's sake, we could barely make rent every month.

Yet whenever I could, I scrounged together the $1.50 it cost to go to a Yankees game with my friends. That $1.50 bought each of us a seat with a view obstructed by a steel pillar, but the seats were on the lower level, along the first or third baseline—the best value in the house. We went to as many doubleheaders as we could to stretch that $1.50 even further. We watched the seats in front of us like hawks so we could swoop in and grab the more premium spots as soon as their occupants left. I usually ate food that I snuck in, because the cost of the ticket itself was all I could afford.

But that was all just fine with me. Those two hours watching the Bombers were a sacred respite from a home life that wasn't exactly ideal. It was a chance to sit among an entire crowd of people who were focused on a shared love. The state-of-the-art facility stood in stark contrast to the ramshackle conditions of my family's small home. I could let my eyes feast on the very stars I read about in the paper and heard about on the radio every day: Mantle. Maris. Yogi. Whitey.

When I was a kid, Yankee Stadium was my personal paradise.

I thought back on those summer days some four decades later, as I drove to the last game that would ever be played at the old Stadium. It was September 20, 2008, and the Yankees were hosting the Baltimore Orioles one final time. It was a big day for my marketing and memorabilia company, Steiner Sports. We were hoping to sell countless items commemorating this day alone.

During the game, I sat in a field level box along the third baseline, with my son Crosby and a few friends. The air was warm, the sky was clear; it was a perfect fall afternoon.

Except for the guy sitting next to me, in the adjacent box.

He looked to be middle-aged, and was wearing tan pants and a blue shirt; he was dressed like he was part of the grounds crew. He pestered me throughout the game, asking me what items my company was going to sell to mark the occasion.

I politely ignored him.

After Mariano Rivera secured the final out of the 5-3 Yankees victory, Mr. Tan Pants leapt out of his seat and ran onto the field. He made it out there before the police even had a chance to set up a barricade.

He ran straight to third base, squatted down, and yanked it out of the ground like a weightlifter hoisting a barbell. Then he ran right back to our section.

As he was climbing back over the railing, I extended my hand as if to help him. Then I lifted the base from under his arm.

Before he realized what had happened, the entire section erupted in a cheer.

"Caught stealing!" someone yelled.

Everyone went crazy.

With all eyes on him, Tan Pants didn't go back to his seat. He fled the section, running up the steps and through the closest exit, before security could get to him. At least he was empty-handed.

I went back to my own seat and sat down. I scanned the stadium, trying to pinpoint those old seats my friends and I used to sit in, the ones with obstructed views.

I couldn't stand by while that guy stole not only a piece of history, but something that now belonged to me.

That's right, me.

When that final game ended, I was responsible for Yankee Stadium and almost everything in it.

But we'll save that story for later.

INTRODUCTION

BEING ALL IN

Not long ago, I was the keynote speaker at an event held for local residents who were out of work or looking to make a career change, at my synagogue in Scarsdale, New York. About 400 people attended. After my talk, the attendees met with representatives from businesses in the area who were hiring. It was a good opportunity to network.

I spoke about my belief that people who are unemployed have to view finding a job as nothing less than a job itself. They must marshal the very same skills and discipline in a job search that they would bring to bear in a job. It's a simple idea, but a difficult mind-set to fully adopt.

After I finished speaking and the audience dispersed, a woman approached me and introduced herself. She explained that she had recently left her job in book publishing to pursue a career as a real estate agent. She had long been passionate about helping people find their dream homes, and renovating and decorating them. She had a good friend with the same passion, and they had started their own real estate agency. They had a lot of clever ideas, and had put a lot of hard work in, not to mention some money. But the business was not yet profitable.

"I don't understand why our ideas aren't working," she said.

She was ambitious and intelligent, but she was discouraged that she was not seeing results faster. Her new venture wasn't as successful as she had anticipated—yet she hadn't been at it that long. But rather than look at her situation as proof that she had more to learn and room to *improve,* she became frustrated.

I see the same kind of thing all the time. People think they're going to start out in an industry, work for a little while, and find instant success. They want the fire, but they don't want to go out and chop the wood.

No matter what business you're in, it takes many years to establish a business, build a reputation for yourself, and achieve success. It usually takes four or five years just to learn your industry and truly master the necessary skills. Then you spend another 5 to 10 utilizing those skills, learning from the experiences you have, and growing your business.

If you think you can enter and succeed in a new industry in only a year or two—you gotta wise up. Because it's just not going to happen.

While I don't think it's more difficult to "make it" today than it was 25 years ago, I do think it's more confusing. We read about young tycoons at start-ups like Zappos and LinkedIn, and we get lost in euphoria when we learn how their companies were instantly valued in the billions, after being around for only a couple of years. We're so starstruck that we fail to consider all the work leading up to those instants.

Throughout this book, I discuss various habits and traits necessary to be successful. But I can tell you right now that the number one requirement, by *far,* is commitment.

The guys who launched Facebook were relentlessly committed to what they were doing for years. Even if it was less than one year from the time Mark Zuckerberg first started programming Facebook to the time it garnered its first major investors, consider the countless years he spent learning computer programming as a kid growing up in White Plains, New York. That part didn't make it into the movie. But it's the most important part.

The innovations that people are generating take the same amount of commitment and passion and time to develop as they always did. However, it takes much less time to bring them to the marketplace. This can confuse people and lead them to believe that success should come faster. And when it does come, while it might come more quickly, so to speak, it certainly doesn't come more easily. In the end, it takes the same amount of work—and time.

What the golden children of the Internet and any other successful entrepreneurs have in common is an incredibly deep commitment to and passion for what they do. (Okay, maybe some of them are also stone cold geniuses; but that's not exactly a teachable character trait.) They are people who are truly "all in" when it comes to their work. They always were. And even when that kind of passion doesn't translate to profound success, it is its own reward. Whether it's directed at a kid, or a lover, or a hobby, or work, passion is what gives us purpose in our lives.

The trick is that while you can feel instantly passionate about another person, or a pastime—and that passion inspires you to commit yourself to its source—when it comes to work, the inverse is actually true. As my good friend Alex Mandossian likes to say, when it comes to work, commitment leads to passion.

To be successful in this world, you gotta grind. You have to wake up every morning and look in the mirror and see someone who's committed to whatever your trade is. You have to find leadership in yourself.

You gotta have the balls to keep at it for years without expecting much in return.

THE GRIND

After graduating from Syracuse University, I had no master plan. I knew I wanted to work in hospitality, but that was it. From there, I transitioned to restaurants. Later, I knew only that I wanted to work with athletes, but I still did not have a sweeping blueprint detailing how it would all work out. During my career, one road led to another too many times to count, and all of a sudden I found myself in a position to take on the biggest deal I could ever imagine—purchasing the demolished Yankee Stadium.

The only master plan I had was to keep grinding it out, to keep throwing myself into every job, every responsibility, every project, and every task—and to welcome new opportunities when they arose. I was always so immersed in the work before me that often I didn't even realize I had done something really significant until I looked back on it later. I was all in. Always.

There's just nothing like looking forward to going to work in the morning. When you feel this, you'll know true passion—and you'll feel that your life has a purpose.

The most common question people ask me about business is, "How did you get started?" I'm never sure where to begin, because I can't trace my success back to a particular place or moment. There wasn't one massive event, or one giant deal; it was more like landing on one island, and later another, and so on—with a lot of treading water in between. The one common thread, the underlying impetus, is commitment. Over the course of almost my entire life, I was committed to countless endeavors. Describing my career makes for a long conversation.

This book is my attempt at having it with you.

NOT BEING ALL IN

There might not be a better example of passion without commitment than Michael Jordan.

I know—relax. I'm not talking about Michael Jordan the basketball player. I'm talking about Michael Jordan the baseball player.

In 1993, when Jordan left the three-time champion Chicago Bulls to pursue a career with the Chicago White Sox, he seemed genuinely passionate about baseball. But with his baseball skills far below the Major League level, the organization wanted him to play on its Double-A squad, the Birmingham Barons. Life in the minors is decidedly unglamorous; these guys play in small towns, for small crowds, for a small salary, and move from city to city by bus. While this kind of life could not have been more opposite to the one to which Jordan was accustomed as the best basketball player on the planet, he accepted the assignment dutifully—which showed he was passionate about baseball.

Jordan played hard the entire season, exhibiting steady if unremarkable progress. And he followed that up by playing for the Scottsdale Scorpions in the Arizona Fall League. But that would be his baseball swan song; Jordan returned to the Bulls the following year. He went on to win three more NBA titles.

If Jordan had been not just passionate about baseball, but also committed, he would have stayed in the minor leagues longer. Most baseball players toil in the minors for several years before making it to "the show."

Michael Jordan is as ferocious and resilient as they come. But when it came to baseball, he had the passion—but not the commitment.

WHAT'S WITH THE WATER IN BROOKLYN?

There's something in the water in Brooklyn. I don't know what it is, but growing up there lights a fire in some people. They start hustling from the time they're little. I'm thinking of people like Jay-Z, Joan Rivers, Woody Allen, and Mel Brooks. Eddie Murphy and Barbra Streisand. Larry King and Rudy Giuliani. Ruth Bader Ginsburg and Mike Tyson. Spike Lee. Joe Torre. Sandy Koufax. Growing up in Brooklyn, you gotta have balls.

My family lived above a kosher butcher shop at 539 Kings Highway, near Ocean Parkway in the Flatbush section of Brooklyn. We were working poor, but we lived in an upper-middle-class neighborhood that had large Syrian Jewish and Italian populations. Many of them were first-generation immigrants. It was a diverse culture, to say the least.

The butcher was called Weingarten & Weiss, and it was glatt kosher, which meant, among other things, that chickens and other animals were slaughtered on the premises. The entire building was always uncomfortably cold, on account of having to store all that raw meat there.

I'd wake up in the morning to the sound of condemned chickens screaming "Bwahhhk!" followed by the sound of the death blow—"Thwack!"

We never saw Weiss, but we saw all too much of Mr. Weingarten, who was also our landlord. Sometimes I think he considered us to be additional slabs of raw meat.

He and I were always in each other's faces: me scolding him over the living conditions and lack of heat in winter; he, deflecting the issue, scolding me about our rent being late. True, the $62 we paid every month wasn't exorbitant. But it was all we could afford, and the welfare check came when it came.

Mr. Weingarten seemed to be particularly fond of turning our heat off on Friday nights, when he would close the store for the Sabbath. During the harshest winters, it got so cold on those weekends that we'd call the police. But when the cops went to his house and ordered him to turn our heat on, Weingarten told them that they had to take his keys, go to the store, and do it themselves. He insisted that he couldn't work on the Sabbath.

Occasionally I would take a hammer and break the lock on the cellar door, to go jump-start the boiler myself. The basement was filled with our fellow tenants: bugs and other animals of unknown origin. I could usually hear them scurry and crackle under my feet.

We probably could have lived in a bigger place, maybe had nicer furniture and more food, if we had lived in a different neighborhood. But our neighborhood had good schools and community centers, and places where my brothers and I could go and be safe while our mom worked. Her logic was that it was better to raise kids in a decent neighborhood—even if it meant stretching every dime to make ends meet.

It took me a long time to realize that the *S* on all the towels in our house stood for *Sheraton*—not for Steiner. After that, I made it my duty to stock up on towels, robes, glasses, and soaps any time we stayed at a hotel. In a way, that was the first time I collected memorabilia.

We certainly knew hunger. We were often on food stamps, a fact I was very embarrassed about, even as a little kid. I've always said I saw the light at a young age—unfortunately, it was the light in the fridge.

My father, Irving Steiner, left when I was five. He suffered from epilepsy, and he was sick most of my childhood. I saw him sporadically until he died, when I was 11.

My mother, Evelyn, basically raised me and my two brothers by herself. Cary is my older brother, I'm the middle child, and Adam is the youngest. The three of us shared a room; Cary had his own bed, and Adam and I shared a bunk bed, with me on top and Adam on the bottom. Three boys, growing up in a single room, smaller than the office I sit in every day.

My mother was a force of nature. She was a brilliant, tireless woman. She was a pretty woman, but she fought with her weight most of her life. At a couple of points, she weighed well over 400 pounds, close to 500 even.

She ran a beauty salon for a long time and was always made up, with gleaming nails. She did amazing things with her hair, changing the color at least once a month, and styling it high and big, like a hedge sculpture. And she usually wore some incredible outfit. You would notice my mother walking down the street from a mile away.

She carried a huge pocketbook with her at all times. She would use it to smuggle home food from weddings and other events. Once we were at a bar mitzvah with an extensive buffet, and there was a problem with the electricity, temporarily leaving us all in the dark. It was a golden opportunity.

"We're at a big buffet with Mom, and the lights are out," Cary said. "We're going to be eating this food for days!"

My mother had a measure of confidence equal to her stature. She had been a real firecracker; as a young woman, she threw herself into political activism and canvassed the city, stumping for Henry Wallace in the 1948 presidential election. She was a magnetic public speaker. But after Wallace lost the election, and the Progressive/American Labor Party ticket went down in flames, she became disillusioned with politics. She turned her attention to her various business ventures.

My mother was constantly promoting her salon, called Evelyn Sachs, after her maiden name. No matter where we were, she'd be marketing herself. We'd walk into a room, and my mother would whisper to us which woman was wearing a wig, which women needed to do something with their look.

"You should stop by the salon," she'd counsel the women in the room. "I could give your hair some color, do your nails—give you a completely new look." She loved getting people excited about changing their looks. She knew her stuff. In those days, there weren't as many manicurists and hair colorists as there are now. But she took classes to learn it all.

My mother had some very clever marketing strategies.

She taught me the value of using your best day to promote your worst day. Beauty parlors were usually packed on Fridays and Saturdays, because women went out those nights. As a result, it was a struggle to get good business going earlier on in the week. So my mother offered a special price for a wash and set on Wednesdays and Thursdays. She never stopped coming up with all sorts of deals, trying to get the place busier during the slow parts of the week.

The salon was two blocks from the Kings Highway stop on the elevated F train. After school I'd linger at the exit of the station, handing out fliers during rush hour. Then I hired some friends to do it. Since most kids didn't want to go hand out fliers for a beauty parlor, I compensated them, paying them in fireworks—which weren't quite legal. Needless to say, I made a little bit of a vig on each kid.

One day, while I was standing underneath the train and giving out the fliers, I thought, "Why just give out fliers for the salon?" I decided to stop by other stores in the neighborhood to offer our services.

"I have three, four, five kids with me every day at rush hour," I told the owners. "We're handing out fliers underneath the train. Do you want us to hand out some fliers for you?" I created my own little side business, making a bit of extra money.

I was always thinking of new ways to pass time and always eager to make an extra buck.

On Saturdays, I worked at the salon, sweeping, cleaning up and doing other chores. Going to the salon was a 10-, sometimes even 12-hour affair for women. They got their nails done, their hair colored, the wash and set; it was a big part of their day. So to make some money, I brought the women their lunches. I took the orders, went to the delis to get the food, and I brought it all back. They gave me good tips.

In reality, despite all the special discounts my mom came up with, the conversation and the camaraderie she kept up in her salon was really what lured women in and brought them back. My mother was warm and gregarious, and often served as a surrogate therapist to her clients. She was always ready to listen to their problems, and to talk them through as long as they needed.

In the salon, I learned that relationships and trust are as important as anything else in business—as crucial as the work that you do or the products you sell. When people feel their best, they *do and act* their best.

I was lucky to get that lesson so early in my life. Back then, men and children rarely went into beauty parlors.

And to this day, I always know which women have colored their hair, and which have their original color. I may not be the best husband in the world, but I at least can tell when my wife has been to the salon.

When my mom was healthy enough, she was always moving a mile a minute, hustling to make an extra buck for my brothers and me. She was incredibly resourceful.

Back when I was younger, airlines used to pay for travel agents to take "familiarization trips" to certain destinations, so they could sell the travel packages from firsthand knowledge. Some summers during high school, I'd watch my mom work two or three phones at the same time, selling warm weather honeymoon trips—just so she could take me and my brothers somewhere. For a few years during our schools' holiday break, we escaped the New York winter by going to Jamaica and other sunny islands. We went on a few cruises in the Caribbean. We even got to go to Disney World right after it opened, in 1971. Even though we were poor, we traveled fairly well, compared to other people in the neighborhood.

And my hair and nails always looked good.

* * * * * * *

Although my mother, my brothers, and I did a good job of making the best out of so many situations, I also went through some dark periods growing up.

During my elementary school years, I spent as much time as possible at the after school center in my Brooklyn neighborhood. The place was amazing; it offered everything from arts and crafts, to music lessons, to basketball leagues for kids whose parents didn't have the time or resources for those types of activities. I particularly liked playing floor hockey there.

The two men who ran the center at that time were Peter Foti and Mel Kerper; Mr. Kerper also happened to be my fifth grade teacher. We had a good relationship, and I was glad to be in his class.

One day we were taking a test when Mr. Kerper called me to his desk. He pulled me in close.

"Brandon," he said. "I want you to know, we took a collection of money, for you to buy new clothes." He handed me an envelope stuffed with bills.

I just stared at him. It completely took my breath away.

"What?"

"You know, we thought you needed some new clothes, so we took a collection."

"How do you know that?" I said.

"Well, you've been wearing the same pants for three weeks in a row," he said. "There's a rip in the right knee."

I wouldn't have noticed if I wasn't even *wearing* pants at that point. I felt naked.

I took the money home. As soon as I saw my mom, I started crying. I told her what happened. I told her I felt humiliated.

"You don't have to worry," she tried to console me. "I was just waiting because I wanted you to lose a little weight before I took you to the store to buy new clothes."

I lay awake in bed that night, thinking about my mother's explanation. It didn't ring true to me. I knew we simply didn't have the money.

It was all I could think about for a few days. I felt embarrassed and sad, but I also felt hungry and determined. I knew my mother was doing the best she could. But I also felt that I needed to be responsible for myself.

"You don't have to worry about me anymore," I announced to my mom a few nights later. "I'm going to make some money. You don't need to buy me any clothes. I got it covered."

I was 10 years old.

That Saturday, I woke up and trolled our street, walking into every store I passed. I canvassed a good two miles of shops, from one end of the street to the other.

"I'll sweep for you," I told the owners. "I'll deliver for you. Anything you need."

Finally, the man who ran a vegetable stand down the block from us took me up on the offer. His store was called Freddy the Fruit Man.

"I could use some help on weekends," the Fruit Man said. "Sweeping up and stocking the vegetables." Shortly after, I began making deliveries for him, as well.

Looking back, it's bittersweet; no 10-year-old should have to go looking for work. But on the other hand, that experience served me well.

That was my first real job.

* * * * * * *

While my memories of my mother are as colorful as she was, my memories of my father are somewhat hazy and gray. The going wisdom in my family was that my mom was always the smartest person in the room, except when Dad was home. But epilepsy had derailed a promising life. He graduated from the Bronx High School of Science and got a scholarship to Columbia, but he had to drop out of college after a couple of years due to health problems. He ended up becoming a shipping clerk in the garment district. By the time I came into his life, the barbiturates my dad had to take to control his seizures had robbed him of much of his vitality.

We saw him on occasional Sundays, and our interactions were usually tense; when we went out with my father, there was always the danger that he might have an attack at any moment. As a little kid, it was incredibly scary and humiliating to be standing on a street corner with my dad when he'd suddenly begin seizing. One time he fell on the sidewalk and broke his jaw; he had to have it wired.

I was a father's dream son: I had a job working before and after school; I was a Cub Scout and Boy Scout; I had a ton of friends; I was crazy about sports, out in the park every day, playing ball. But my dad's health problems and fractured relationship with my mom prevented him from becoming engaged in my life. It didn't help that he was more into music and art than sports. Those weren't two of my favorites.

I remember liking his drawings, though; he could always draw really well. And he could be very funny. He was kind of corny, but when he was feeling well, my dad was capable of really making us laugh. But my brother Cary was a lot closer to him than I was.

When my dad passed away at the age of 48, there were only eight people at his funeral—that included the four of us, and his sister; so you can do the math. At a Jewish funeral, you're supposed to have a minyan, which means at least 10 Jewish adults have to be present. We had to grab a couple of passersby just to say the prayers at the side of my dad's grave. There was barely any service at all, really. It was raining. We weren't there for very long.

My father's death had a profound effect on me. I felt terrible that he wasn't missed by more people. I remember thinking that I could never let that happen to me.

I think it's a healthy exercise to think about who will miss you when you die. What have you accomplished while hanging out on this planet? What kind of effect have you had on others—and on yourself? What are you leaving behind? Will our world be better off because you were here?

I do have fond memories of my dad taking me bowling several times, probably the only sport we ever did together. He took me to a place called Spa Bowl on Coney Island Avenue, where every lane had one red pin mixed in with the white ones. If the red pin was set in the very front, and you bowled a strike in that frame, you got a cherry Coke on the house. The two of us won our fair share of sodas.

As he taught me to bowl on those sunny days, my dad was fluid and graceful. Those were times we could be athletic together, however fleetingly. So when my wife, Mara, and I built our house a number of years ago, I made sure that we installed a bowling lane in the basement—to remember Dad by.

Though certainly better off than my father, my mother was rarely in perfect health herself. Her weight was a dark cloud on almost every aspect of her life. She initiated many discussions about her dying with my brothers and me, even when we were young. She'd make sure she had our attention, and then launch into her go-to hypothetical.

"If I die . . . " she'd say to us, then provide specific instructions for money, the apartment, and taking care of each other. Death hovered around her.

My mother was one of the first people to get gastric bypass surgery, in 1970. The operation caused a lot of complications; it was scary. She was in the hospital for about five months, and my brothers and I had no idea what was going on. Our Aunt Lee lived four miles away, with my mother's father, and she kept a bit of an eye on us. We took a bus to my grandfather's house for dinner many nights. My aunt meant well, but she was not the warmest person. She resented having to look after us, and we felt it.

I know she had her own issues to deal with, but I've always had difficulty understanding why Aunt Lee didn't put on a sunnier face for us. If she had assumed her caretaker role with a little more generosity in her heart, it would have made a world of difference to my brothers and me. And the whole thing would have been easier—and maybe even gratifying and enjoyable—for her.

> If you do somebody a favor, why not do it in good faith, with a positive attitude? If she had been a bit kinder, I would have built Aunt Lee a statue by now. Instead of feeling ambivalent about her my whole life.

It was a very troubling time, and at one point, my mother almost died. Her liver was on the brink of failure. All of a sudden we were rushed to the hospital, totally bewildered.

Children under 12 weren't allowed in the intensive care unit, which was on one of the upper floors. But since the doctors thought my mom was likely to die, they lifted her out of bed, plopped her in a wheelchair, and took her to the lobby to say goodbye to us.

I'll never forget how my mother looked at that moment, slumped in that chair, practically falling over the side. It was very sad. She was so depleted. I felt like I was looking at death.

That night, there was a lot of tension back at my grandfather's place. I remember getting into a screaming fight with him and Aunt Lee, who worried that my brothers and me were about to be foisted on her, permanently.

Somehow, my mother made a miraculous recovery. I still don't know how.

"I was about to pass to the other side," she liked to say to us. "But the thought of Aunt Lee raising you brought me back."

Despite the traumatic complications of the weight-loss surgery, a year later, my mother was set on losing still more weight, so she checked herself into an in-patient weight loss clinic at the hospital. She was away another few months. In a span of three years, my mother wasn't home for over a year. It was just my brothers and me, living in that little apartment with virtually no parental supervision, other than my mother calling sometimes. Even though Cary was the oldest, I basically took on the role of running the house—as much as anyone was running anything. I did most of the shopping, bill paying, cooking, and other essential chores. Many times I had to take my mother's checkbook to write out the rent check myself, then beg the landlord to hold it for a few days while we paid for some other necessities.

I even made trips to the local Con Ed office when we were unable to pay our electric bill, to plead for an extension. I had to stand at a distance from the counter so I could angle my head to see the lady behind it. I begged her not to cut off our power.

Having to take on so many responsibilities at a young age was amazing training—the kind that makes running a company feel almost easy. But those years caused profound problems for me, Cary, and Adam, because we had too much independence. We never had anyone looking over our shoulders to help us with our homework, make sure we stayed out of trouble, or show us how to do the right thing. Drugs and alcohol found both of my brothers too soon. But it was different for me. From a very young age, I learned to find more productive things to keep me busy through all of the family drama. That was how I first came to fall in love with sports—it offered an escape from my home life. On any given day, I did everything I could either to go to a game, watch a game, or play in a game. When my friends and I got too old to play in the schoolyard, many of them transferred that energy to girls, drugs, or alcohol. But I wasn't yet into any of that.

Instead, I started going to the Jewish Community House of Bensonhurst every day after school. The JCH had a pool, a basketball court, and everything else you could think of. It also had a small tuition requirement that I couldn't afford, but my mom found a way to take care of that.

The executive director of the JCH was a former Lincoln High School gym teacher named Milt Gold. Milt was a local legend of sorts, having served as a father figure to hundreds, if not thousands, of Brooklyn kids in his decades running the JCH. In addition to coaching, he took a real interest in improving the lives of young people, encouraging them in their hobbies and passions, and steering them away from dangerous or illicit behaviors. My mom went to him personally to implore him to spend some time with me. He took a real liking to me, and effectively gave me a scholarship to attend the JCH for free.

I'd run there the minute school ended, and play ball right up to dinner. Sometimes I even went back there after I ate, and played until they had to kick me out and lock up for the night. For a couple of years, I was also a forward on the JCH's basketball club team. We played teams from other community centers from all over the tri-state area. Milt always made sure we had some of the nicest uniforms in Brooklyn. That might sound like a small thing, but to a kid like me, who could never afford nice clothes, putting on that jersey was like becoming someone else for an evening—someone deserving, and special, and cared for. I'll always be grateful to Milt for those particular memories of my adolescent years.

When I wasn't at the JCH, I was spending time at my friends' houses, each of which had the advantage of a potential meal. I was usually starving. I could always count on Charlie Marcus's place to have a big home-cooked dinner, while David Badar always had money for Chinese food or pizza. There were a number of parents in the neighborhood that looked after my brothers and me when they had the time.

I worked at making friends anywhere I could, with people from all different social circles and ethnic backgrounds. I was friends with the Italians, the Syrians, the Jewish kids; I was friends with the nerds and the jocks. I was able to get along with folks from all different walks of life; I needed to keep busy, and that meant being able to move between groups effortlessly.

For a long time while we were growing up, my mother took in boarders—random people she knew who were passing through Brooklyn for one reason or another. She felt that she was accruing good karma hosting these transients. I welcomed the houseguests, because I felt there was so much I could learn from them. I would ask them endless questions about their lives, their jobs, the things they'd seen.

That was one of the great things about Brooklyn. You had to have balls growing up there, but being part of such a diverse community of people—all trying to get by—also gave you a big heart. On a daily basis, I interacted with and relied upon so many different kinds of people that it was impossible *not* to develop a strong sense of empathy. Now, kids can go on the web and discover hundreds of lives unlike their own. In Brooklyn, we got that experience every time we got on the subway. It was priceless preparation for adult life, and for my business.

Understanding different types of people—being able to channel their wants and needs—gives you an edge in business. Having a network of friends with very diverse personalities, from all different backgrounds, can lead to amazing opportunities that might not otherwise come up.

THE SECRET OF 'WHAT ELSE?'

There are two things people from the old neighborhood say about me—they didn't know any kid as poor as I was, and they didn't know any kid who worked as hard as I did.

After my tenure with Freddy the Fruit Man, I got a paper route delivering the *Daily News* on my bike—29 dailies and 37 Sunday papers.

But I needed more. The *News* had a contest for the paperboys that ran every week; the kid who opened the most new accounts won a box of candy bars—24 bars! To a hungry kid like me, that sounded like a steak dinner at Peter Luger.

But how would I open enough new accounts to guarantee victory?

Every morning, I walked by some big apartment buildings on my way to school. There had to be a hundred apartments in each building, dozens of new accounts for the taking.

One morning I decided to enter one of the buildings, knock on a few doors, and gauge interest. At the first door, an elderly lady answered.

"Would you like to buy the *Daily News* from me?" I asked. "I can deliver it every day."

"Why should I do that?" she countered. "I can go to the store every day, and it costs me the same eight cents. But if I have you deliver it, I have to tip you, too."

Getting the paper delivered didn't cost extra, but she was right—you were expected to tip the paperboy. The *News* paid me a small fee for delivering papers on the route, but most of my money came from tips.

When I got home that day, I told the story to my mother.

"Besides selling them a newspaper," she asked, "What else could you do for these people?"

The next morning, I knocked on the same lady's door.

"Would you like to buy the *Daily News* from me?" I asked. "I can deliver it every day."

"Why should I do that?" she said again. "I can go to the store every day, and it costs me the same eight cents. If I have you deliver it, I have to tip you, too."

It was like déjà vu all over again. But this time I was ready.

"Because if you get the paper delivered from me every day," I said, "I'll bring you milk twice a week, and I'll bring you bagels on Sunday."

In those days, there weren't bagel stores all over the city, but I lived right by one. Having a source of bagels nearby was kind of a big deal.

"Wow," the lady said. "You would do that for me?"

"Yeah, I'll bring you the bagels on Sunday," I said. "And on Thursdays, when you pay me for the *News*, you can pay me for the bagels, too."

She signed up. One new account.

I went around to the rest of the building, and neighboring buildings, hitting up everyone with that bagel rap. Before I knew it, I was delivering over a 100 dailies and over 150 Sunday papers. Of course, I was also delivering around a hundred gallons of milk every week and over a hundred bagels every Sunday.

I'd wake up at 6 a.m. to do my route every morning during the week, and be finished by seven. On Sundays, I had to make two separate trips with a shopping cart to carry all the bagels and papers I had to deliver. The paper's sections came in different batches, and each paperboy had to collate them. Sometimes my mom would help me by waking up early and putting the Sunday paper together for me.

Most people have to wait until after college to find a job they're passionate about. I was lucky to be passionate about that paper-bagel-milk route at such a young age.

And I constantly won the candy bar contest. I was a dynasty!

The kids who focused solely on signing new accounts didn't seem to fare as well as I did, a fact that supports one of my favorite maxims: If you want more business, don't pay attention to the money. Pay attention to the thing that *makes* the money. I concentrated on potential customers—on *people*—rather than on accounts. This sounds like semantics, but it's not. People eat bagels, accounts don't. But in turn, those happy customers signed new accounts.

After a few weeks, the guy who ran the bagel factory started to notice me. How could he not? I was buying more bagels than anyone else. One day he pulled me aside.

"How would you like to work for me in the mornings?" he asked.

"I already have this paper route in the mornings," I told him. "I don't have any spare time."

"You can work for me two days a week, 4:30 to 7:00, and you can deliver your papers a little bit later those mornings," he explained. "You'll earn five extra hours of pay every week."

What the heck. I was a young, hungry kid. Besides—when else would I be able to do stuff like this?

So one weekday and one weekend day, I woke up at four in the morning. And I learned how to bake bagels.

A couple of months after I started, the night baker quit. The timing was perfect. I got the promotion to night baker after only a couple of months of that 4 a.m. *chazerai*. My new job paid me $1.50 an hour, which wasn't bad in those days. And the job was relatively easy. That was one of my first lessons in luck being the residue of hard work.

My mother's words kept echoing in my head. "What else could you do for these people?"

One night I came home from baking bagels, very excited.

"I have a great idea, Mom," I said. "I want to get a food truck, and every Saturday and Sunday, I want to load it up with bagels, cream cheese, lox, and donuts—everything people need for their Saturday and Sunday morning breakfast—and deliver all of it. The neighborhood folks won't have to schlep around to get breakfast. They can sleep in a little later, and I'll earn a little more money. We'll put a giant bagel on top of the truck, so people will remember it."

"Brandon, it's a really good idea," she said. "But there's one problem. You're 15. You can't drive."

It hadn't even occurred to me before she said it. That's just not how my mind worked. It didn't register obstacles.

Unfortunately, my mom's way of finding the *What Else* could occasionally push the boundaries of creativity and become predatory. Like many of my Jewish friends, I long looked forward to becoming a Bar Mitzvah when I turned 13, with the attendant ceremony at synagogue, and—more importantly—the reception.

But while we were planning the party, which was going to take place at a hotel outside the city, I voiced my concern that we didn't have enough money to pay for it.

"Brandon," my mom said with a soft voice, "what do you think we're going to do with the money everyone will give you?"

The next day at school, I made sure to stress to my friends how fond I was of three-dimensional gifts.

MY FIRST AUTOGRAPH

This year is the 25th anniversary of Steiner Sports, and I think that if I had to sum up our business in one sentence—one thought—it would read: Steiner Sports is the number-one collector of autographs in the world. In some 26 years, we have bought and sold almost 20 million autographs—and set up over 35,000 athlete appearances.

And tens of thousands of autographs later, I'm pleased to say I'll never forget the first autograph I ever acquired.

It was 1969; I was 11 years old. One summer day I was hanging out on the street corner with three older boys, including Bobby Pertsas, who would later become Baseball Commissioner of New York City's Public School Athletic League (the PSAL), and my friend Henry Delgadio. We were debating whether the Yankees or Mets were the better team that year, a discussion that prompted someone to propose that we go to that day's Yankees game at the Stadium. Honored by the older kids' invitation to join them, I ran home to get my mother's permission—and financial backing.

"Mom," I squealed, "can I go with them? Please!"

She must have sensed that this was a special opportunity for me, because my mother barely hesitated.

"Here's five dollars," she said, handing me one of the bills she had on her. "Have a good time. But bring me back the change."

The subway cost 15 cents each way. And after we got to the Stadium, after a quick trip to the ticket window, Bobby announced that he had landed a special deal for us.

(continued)

(continued)

"You're not gonna believe this," he said. "They just released some tickets. I got us seats right near the on-deck circle!"

"How much are they?" I said.

"Four bucks each," he replied.

That was a bit steep, but what choice did I have? We all handed over our money. I had already spent $4.30. And once we got in, of course I had to buy a hot dog and scorecard. Another 25 cents.

When we got to our seats, the balance sheet in my mind was wiped away by the smell of the green grass, which seemed to be wafting up from right under my nose, and the vision of Yankee Joe Pepitone signing autographs only a few feet away.

Eventually we got Pepitone to come over and sign our programs; at our beckoning, he even called Tom Tresh to come over and sign for us as well.

I had never before been that close to a Major League field, let alone Major League players, let alone Yankees, let alone had the pleasure of two of them signing my program before my very eyes.

Needless to say, I was in a state of ecstasy the entire game. I have no idea what happened on the field the rest of the game—let alone to the remaining 70 cents I had on me. And I'm sure I didn't much care.

But as soon as I walked in the door after I got back home that night, my mom's voice rang out.

"Where's my change?" she said.

Eyes beaming, I explained the magic of the afternoon. How priceless the experience was. Joe Pepitone! Tom Tresh! They signed for me. I had their autographs—two real live Yankees! But my mom was not impressed.

"You spent four dollars on a baseball ticket?!" she said.

She ran out of the house, down to the aforementioned street corner, where the older boys had resumed the day's earlier discussion.

"Where's my change!" she screamed. "Where's my money! How dare you!"

Of course I was petrified.

Of course she got her money back.

* * * * * * *

(continued)

(*continued*)

Four years later, I found out that when the Yankees traveled to play the Red Sox, they stayed at the Sheraton in Boston. Thanks to her travel agency connections, my mom was able to get a good rate at Sheraton hotels. I begged her to take me to Boston one weekend, when the Yankees were playing a series at Fenway. I was sure I'd meet some of my heroes if I could just spend a couple of nights in the same hotel as them.

We drove up on a Thursday; we were going to explore Boston on Friday, go to the game Saturday afternoon, and drive back after the game. But as we were wrapping up our sightseeing Friday, I was able to talk my mom into letting me go to that night's game as well.

I'll never forget the first time I walked into Fenway Park. It was unbelievable. I had managed to score an amazing ticket from a scalper outside the stadium; my seat was five rows behind the Yankees dugout. I was yelling to my favorite players throughout the entire game. It annoyed the hell out of the Sox fans around me, but I didn't care. I didn't think I'd ever be that close to my beloved team again, and I couldn't let the opportunity pass me by. I focused my attention on Thurman Munson, the great catcher and legendary Yankees captain.

"Thurman! Thurman! Thurman!" I kept screaming. "What's up Thurman! Thurmaaaan!"

But he didn't even glance at me.

After the game, I sulked back to the Sheraton, disappointed I hadn't gotten anyone's attention. When I got back to the hotel, I waited in the lobby a bit, hoping I'd catch the team coming back from the ballpark. But I gave up after a little while; no one was coming.

Then, after I got in the elevator to go up to my room, a giant arm knifed through, preventing the doors from closing at the last second. The doors reopened, and I practically fainted; the arm belonged to Thurman Munson.

"What do you want from me?" he bellowed. "Why were you yelling my name for two hours straight?"

Trembling, I explained I was a huge fan of his, and that I really only wanted his autograph. He laughed, and happily obliged, signing my program from the game.

Several years later, in 1979, when Thurman died in a plane crash at 32, I know I wasn't the only Yankee fan crying. But I also felt so grateful to have had that experience with him. He was a great man.

LIFE, DEATH, AND SODA

DEWEY HIGH SCHOOL

"You're going to be like Donald Trump one day," my mom used to tell me. "You have that same fearless attitude in you."

My bond with my mother was rooted in a shared passion for business more than anything else. Most of our conversations were about money—how little we had ourselves, the many ways other people made theirs, what personal qualities made someone successful in business, and why some businesses took off while others failed. That was the language we shared.

By the time I was a teenager, my mother was certain that one day I'd run a business. I had inherited her nose for it. She wasn't sure what kind of business I'd run—it could have been anything from a shoe store to an airline—but she had no doubt I'd be at the top of it.

It gave me confidence when she referred to me as the next Donald Trump; it inspired me to work hard, to fulfill her image of me.

Young people have incredibly malleable minds. Repeat almost anything to them enough, and eventually they'll begin to believe it. This can cut both ways. If you constantly tell a child, "I wish I never had you," he'll start to believe he's worthless, if for no other reason than your insistence. Encourage him consistently, and he'll believe in himself just as blindly.

My mother wanted to give me the necessary tools to take our shared entrepreneurial spirit further than she could—so she sent me to John Dewey High School, in Coney Island. Named after psychologist, intellectual, and philosopher John Dewey, it had opened just a couple of years earlier, in 1969, and it was getting a lot of press for being a progressive school. John Dewey was renowned for his work in education and social reform, as well as the books he published on educational theory, in which he endorsed an experience and inquiry-based approach to learning. He emphasized real world skills and social maturity. In other words, Dewey liked to cut through the crap.

Naturally, Dewey High was based on the man's philosophies. It was experimental. All the classes were pass/fail, under the guise that students would learn more if we weren't busy competing for grades. Foreign language and technology were important subjects, but the school housed robust art and music departments as well, and offered Shakespeare and journalism classes. Among other advances, Dewey was the first New York City high school to offer a marine biology class.

At first, I was reluctant about going to school there, because Dewey didn't have sports teams—and sports were such a huge part of my life. After all, I was going to play professionally one day! I didn't see how I could have a career in sports if I didn't attend a high school with a sports program. But my mother saw this as a good thing. She wasn't into skills or hobbies that didn't directly lead to earning money; she thought the lack of sports at Dewey would naturally steer me to more practical arenas.

"Brandon, I know you love basketball," my mom said, "but you're probably never going to be taller than 5'7". I don't think the NBA is going to take you."

I was sold.

PLAYING YOUR BEST CARDS

My mother knew I was never going to be a wildly successful athlete or academic—that my innate intelligence was emotional, not intellectual. She sent me to Dewey to sharpen my natural skills, because she knew this was the most effective way for me to find success in life. My close friend Mariano Rivera would have appreciated her stance. The Yankees closer is fond of saying that people should focus on developing their strengths, as opposed to strengthening their weaknesses.

That mentality has certainly served him well. Early in his career, coaches used to go over scouting reports with Mo and tell him to avoid throwing his fearsome cutter to certain batters, who excelled at hitting fastballs.

"What was I going to do?" Mo says. "The cut fastball was my only pitch! I couldn't let that stuff get in my head."

Mo didn't want to do something he didn't excel at—like pitching a changeup—to keep him from doing what he did exceptionally well and what he had confidence in: throwing his cutter. He shook off the scouts' advice and stuck to his signature pitch—for his whole career.

All it got Mo was the all-time regular season and postseason saves records, 5 Relief Man of the Year awards, 12 All-Star appearances, and a World Series and ALCS MVP award—to say nothing of unanimous recognition as the greatest closer in baseball history.

Not a bad return on a single strength.

Students at Dewey could join any number of 60 different clubs, which operated on a more professional level than those at other high schools. Since there were no team sports, the school put all of its extracurricular funding into the student groups. Theater, art, dance, debate, cooking, chess, prayer groups—we had it all, and they were first-rate. I knew exactly how much money went to each club, because I was school treasurer in my senior year.

I had run for student government with my friend, Cliff Savage, in the junior year elections; he ran for vice-president, and I ran for treasurer. We made buttons that said NOTHING COULD BE FINER THAN SAVAGE AND STEINER. And WHAT COULD BE MORE DANDY THAN CLIFF AND BRANDY?

Unfortunately, Cliff lost his race, but I was elected treasurer. Along with a faculty advisor, I appropriated money to all student groups. In the process I learned even more about empathy—not to mention politics.

Dewey also offered a co-op program, which some people called a "four and one." Students would attend school four days a week, and then go to a "regular job" on the other day. It was a very formative program.

As part of the four and one, during my junior year, I worked in the emergency room of Maimonides Hospital, in Borough Park, Brooklyn. Cliff had chosen to work in the hospital to please his father, who was a renowned ophthalmologist; he begged me to go with him, and I agreed.

We basically served as orderlies, rotating through different hospital departments and helping the doctors and nurses with whatever was needed—the smaller tasks that tended to slip through the cracks during an average day.

Our first day, we were assigned to the emergency room. While there, a young girl who was around our age was rushed in on a gurney, hooked up to all sorts of tubes and pumps. Her name was Gina. There was a team of doctors and nurses flying around her, and her father was by her side. Gina was suffering an allergic reaction to penicillin, which the hospital had given her to address something else. As they were treating her in the ER, Gina went into cardiac arrest—right in front of Cliff and me.

The scene was indescribable. Then her heart stopped beating.

Cliff and I were given the assignment of bringing Gina's body down to the morgue. Gina's father came down with us, his hand still clutching his daughter's. I'll never forget the elevator ride down with Cliff, and Gina, and her dad. He was crying uncontrollably, repeating her name.

Despite the fact that it was a harrowing experience, it gave me some perspective. The Steiners weren't the only family that dealt with sickness and death. It was an object lesson in the expression: "Where there's life, there's hope."

The next few months provided Cliff and me countless additional lessons; thankfully, most of them were less stark than that first one. The hospital was its own city; we got to see what went into running it from the inside out. We saw what the doctors and nurses endured in an average day—and in an average week—as opposed to the hour-long slices most of us experience when we go in for appointments. There was no shortage of authentic heroes among the staff. Watching them in action, Cliff and I learned the value of teamwork and trust, and persistence and commitment. The patients taught us about sacrifice and faith.

I *never* would have thought to go work in a hospital on my own; I had had more than enough of them on account of my mother. But in the end, I was so glad that I had done it. It usually pays to go outside of your comfort zone, and the further out you go, the bigger the payoff. I couldn't have gotten those experiences anywhere else.

MY FIRST COLLECTIBLES

It was actually a personal injury that led to my first foray into the world of sports collectibles.

When I was a little kid, soda was sold only in glass bottles. During every shipment, a few bottles per truck usually got jostled around too much and exploded or shattered. The delivery or store men would notice and replace them; these bottles rarely reached anyone's home. But one such bottle that slipped through the cracks ended up in our house.

One day when I was two years old, I was playing with a Pepsi bottle when it abruptly shattered in my hands. A glass shard flew into my face, ripping through my left eyelid. Blood was everywhere.

My mother rushed me to the emergency room of Kings County Hospital. The resident who examined me told her that while my eye and my sight were not in danger, the nature of the wound might leave that part of my face with a serious scar.

"Who would be the best doctor to do the stitches for something like this?" my mom asked him.

"That would be the chief of plastic surgery," the doctor answered. "But he's not here right now, so we'll have to call an attending physician."

"When will the chief of plastic surgery be back?"

"He won't be in until tomorrow," the doctor said. "At least another 12 hours. Maybe longer."

Holding a toddler in her lap who was bleeding out of his eye, my mother was faced with a choice. She could have me stitched up, cleaned up, and back home in little time. That was the safe play. But she knew that this scar would be with me my entire life, in a prominent location. She wanted to make sure that the best doctor possible did the stitches.

"We will wait for the chief surgeon," she said.

Just because we were poor didn't mean that we were less worthy of the best medical care. We waited.

It has faded a lot, but I still have the scar 54 years later: a half-inch streak under my left eye, like the track of a tear. For a

(continued)

(*continued*)

long time now, it's been just deep enough to be noticeable in good light, but not enough to alter the look of my face. It doesn't feel as unsightly to me as it did while I was growing up and, with all the history behind it, I've come to appreciate the scar.

Had we not waited for the chief surgeon, I don't know that it would look so different. But I'm glad my mother had that patience, because there was a lot at stake. It was my face after all!

"Better to wait three days for a good doctor," my mother would say, "than see an inexperienced doctor right away."

The plastic surgery notwithstanding, the scar was somewhat prominent for most of my childhood, and for a long time, my equilibrium was a little off. My head would always tilt at a slight angle when I walked.

My mother hired a lawyer and filed a lawsuit against Pepsi. The case dragged on for years. It went on so long, in fact, that a settlement wasn't reached until I was in high school. By that time, the case had wound up in the hands of a lawyer named Sid Loberfeld, who also happened to represent several professional athletes, including a few New York Mets. Sid got us a settlement of about $5,600, $4,000 of which was placed in a savings account for me.

A couple of years later—in between my high school graduation and my first year of college at Syracuse—I got into a car accident with a couple of friends in Sussex, New Jersey, where I was working as a camp counselor. I was in the front middle seat, and my head hit the rearview mirror. Amazingly, we were all okay—except that I had reinjured my eye.

Now I had to deal with the car insurance company. I enlisted Sid, and this time he brokered a settlement of $10,000. Again, the money was put into my savings account. As a bonus, Sid gave me some sports memorabilia he had picked up from dealing with his athlete clients, including ticket stubs from the 1969 World Series of the "Miracle Mets," old baseball programs, and a baseball autographed by a major leaguer whose name I unfortunately can't recall.

At the time, I had no way of knowing that years later, that insurance settlement, and the settlement from Pepsi, would play key roles in my fledgling business.

Syracuse

My father graduated from the Bronx High School of Science at 16, earning a scholarship to Columbia in the process. But he still needed money for room and board, so he had to work full time while attending school. He kept it up for two years, until he developed pneumonia, after which he started having epileptic seizures. The doctors told his family that my father's body couldn't take the stress it was under; he had to either quit school or quit working to maintain his health. His mother refused to aid him financially; he was forced to quit Columbia, and his life began a steady descent. My mother had briefly attended Hunter College, but never made it through.

My brother Cary was the intellect of the family. He was a writer and a poet, with exceptional SAT scores. But he was a renegade; he didn't care about high school and struggled to achieve a 65 average. So Cary's college prospects were bleak. He went to the State University of New York at Geneseo for a year and a half before dropping out.

Even though I was only an average student at Dewey, it became apparent that I was the best hope to be the family's first college graduate. My mother was determined to see that through.

When it came time to look at schools, my friend David Badar and I decided we would take a road trip to visit three—Utica, Syracuse, and Ithaca. Nowadays kids visit any number of colleges. Back then, it was common to apply to state schools and only go on one trip to visit them.

David and I left at midnight one Friday night, so we would arrive at our destination early Saturday morning—saving money on a hotel. Utica was the first stop. We got there at four o'clock in the morning, and took a little nap. When we woke up around six o'clock, it had snowed so much that our car was buried up to the windows. We dug ourselves out, and drove to a gas station, where we changed and "spruced up" a little in the bathroom. Then we drove to the campus. The roads were practically impossible to navigate. The campus itself was almost invisible—completely buried in snow. Utica was a very small town. It wasn't for me.

Our next stop was Syracuse. I knew as soon as I set foot on the campus that it was the one. There was a thick blanket of snow there too, but all the buildings and walkways were perfectly plowed; the place seemed to thrive in the inclement weather. There was so much going on; it was like a self-contained city. I felt right at home.

As we walked around, I kept thinking, "This is unbelievable."

I had an entrance interview scheduled at Syracuse that day. As I went into it, I thought, "I don't want this to be the last time I see this place."

Then I had the interview of my life.

"I don't have any money," I told the admissions counselor. "My SAT scores are kind of low, and my grades are pass/fail. But I've been working full time since I started high school. I've contributed to every student club I could fit in my schedule. I've been involved with so many activities I can barely remember them all. If you give me this opportunity, I promise you I will use every inch of this school. You will never regret letting me in."

As I said that, I also said a silent prayer that the counselor would not look further into my SAT score. I got a 760—combined math and reading comprehension. It was important that she took my word that the score was "kind of low," as opposed to discovering for herself that it was "worrisome."

I felt that I had made a strong impression on the counselor; she really took a liking to me. She asked me question after question about my life, family, and experiences. I could tell she wasn't going to take my application and just put it in a pile; she'd go to bat for me.

This was the first time I came to understand how important it is to make an impression *on* someone, instead of simply impressing them in the moment. It's a subtle difference, but an important one.

> When you impress someone, they admire and respect you, but that might be the extent of their feelings. Imagine a well-dressed man walking into a business meeting; his style and confidence may impress the people there. But will they think about him while they're eating dinner or at work the next day?
>
> On the other hand, you leave a *mark* on someone when you make an impression. You facilitate a mutual emotional investment. Picture the aforementioned well-dressed man complimenting someone in the room on his work or even appearance. That's something he'll remember later on.

I realized early on that making an impression is a combination of impressing someone and asking them *What Else?*, offering them that little extra something that no one else will bring to the table. That's what I did with the Syracuse admissions counselor.

And I got in—to all three schools, in fact.

Of course, once I got into the three, I had to apply to more. I was on a roll. The deadlines hadn't passed, and I was playing with house money. I had a student aid waiver, so I didn't have to pay any of the application fees.

I applied to a few top-tier schools, like Duke and the University of Pennsylvania.

I figured, what did I have to lose? It's important to take chances in life—even ones that come with long odds.

I didn't get into a single one.

* * * * * * * *

Syracuse was the most expensive college in New York State. On the surface, it didn't seem like the most likely place for a poor kid like me to go to school. On the other hand, the way my mother operated, it was the logical place. I needed a ton of student aid, and she felt the richest school would be able to give me more support than any other college.

Indeed, Syracuse offered me a generous amount of student aid.

I enrolled and moved up there in the fall of 1977.

SKILLS BEFORE BILLS

David Badar's family ran an Odd Job Store in lower Manhattan that sold various knickknacks. I worked there over Christmas breaks during high school, selling fake Christmas trees. After our senior year, David's father offered me $125 per week to work in the store over the summer, which would have amounted to a total salary of well over $1,000. I spent the prior summer working at Camp Sussex as a waiter in the cafeteria. I had long planned to work there again—making $150 for the *entire* summer—but the Badars' lucrative offer made for a difficult decision.

Although I was already committed to Sussex, I knew I could get out of it if I wanted. But I liked working at camp; I spent nine great summers in a row there, first as a camper, then as an employee. And not only did I like it, but that summer I was scheduled to work in the kitchen. It was a chance to work under Alzie Jackson, the head cook and a camp legend. Alzie was highly regarded as a mentor. I had done a lot of cooking in my life, but I knew that working in the kitchen at camp the whole summer under Alzie would bring that skill to a whole new level.

So instead of choosing the position where I would make more money, I chose the job that promised to make me feel productive and give me practical skills.

It wasn't easy working in that kitchen. Every day, as Alzie's helper, I was the first to arrive at work in the morning (6 a.m.); and as a dishwasher, I was the last to leave at night (7:30 p.m.). I worked

(continued)

(continued)

12- to 14-hour days, with only three days off the entire summer. The average temperature in the kitchen was 90 degrees. It definitely wasn't sitting in a hammock and drinking lemonade.

But sure enough, by the end of that summer, I had mastered dishwashing, bussing, and working the grill and griddle. And as I would learn soon enough, sometimes it pays to choose skills over the bigger paycheck.

A few weeks after I began Syracuse, it became obvious that I'd need to take a work-study job if I was to afford any sort of normal student life there. Since most of my friends didn't have to work, I was a little bummed out about it. However, the school gave me a few options, and I chose to work in the dorm cafeteria. I figured that I could at least utilize my kitchen experience, and maybe earn a higher salary by virtue of my relevant skills. Not to mention meeting every girl in the dorm. (Talk about turning a negative into a positive.)

At the beginning of my junior year at Syracuse, I was elected treasurer of my fraternity, Fiji. That experience was a great lesson on how to allocate money, piggybacking on what I had learned as treasurer at Dewey. And it didn't take long for me to learn another lesson in politicking, either.

When I became treasurer, the soda machine in the frat house basement dispensed cans for 25 cents. But one day I was going over our books, and I discovered that the sodas were costing us 26 cents apiece to buy. We were losing a penny every time some guy stumbled downstairs and bought a soda. This small discrepancy was adding up. Raising the price of each soda to a mere 30 cents would make a significant difference to the fraternity's finances. So I proposed this increase at the next house meeting.

I could not have imagined the outcry this suggestion would inspire. I had to sit there and listen to two hours of anger, and fear, and disbelief—over a 30-cent soda. By the end of the meeting, I felt as if I was about to be the victim of a coup d'état.

"When my grandfather was at Syracuse," one brother said, "he chose this frat above all others for the 25-cent soda."

"I have a stack of quarters in my room," another guy said. "I started it because I knew that when I felt thirsty, I could take a quarter and go downstairs and get a soda."

There was a silence.

"Now I have to make a stack of nickels," he continued, "in addition to the quarters."

"What if you have a girl over and you want two sodas?" someone said. "You might even need dimes!"

"You're planning on us making money *off of ourselves*?"

"How capitalistic can you get?!"

"We should absorb that money."

It was intense. It was Occupy the Soda Machine.

I came home one day and some of my belongings had been chucked on the lawn outside the house. To send a message.

While the whole thing seemed irrational, it was a teachable moment. When you make a change that affects your team—no matter how insignificant it seems—you first have to get people on board, whether it's your employees, your friends, or your family. But especially if it's your frat brothers. This supports my earlier claim that putting people at ease and compelling them to trust you are an essential first step in business and in life.

Change is always difficult for some people, no matter how small. A good leader will make his team comfortable with a change before he puts it in place. It doesn't matter if the change is obviously the right way to go. There is no sense in being right if you can't get it right.

In the end, I couldn't get the soda increase approved. For all I know, they're down to 10 cents by now.

* * * * * * *

My mother encouraged me to major in accounting at Syracuse. She felt it was the most practical skill for me to learn, which made sense to me.

I did well enough the first couple of years, but I began to struggle when I had to take intermediate accounting during my junior year. Some of the more complex formulas and concepts just weren't sinking in.

One Friday night, I was sitting at my desk in my room at Fiji, trying to study. My accounting notes were scattered around me like fallen leaves. The giant textbook sat open in front of me, inscrutable as the Dead Sea Scrolls. I felt lost.

Below me, I heard music, and chatter, the sounds of cabinets opening and closing, and furniture being rearranged. The house was going to throw a massive party in a couple of hours. I looked forward to drinking with my frat brothers—and hopefully some cute girls—and leaving intermediate accounting behind. I'd deal with it Sunday night.

I began to straighten up my workspace. As I did this, something dawned on me. If I felt anxious about accounting early on a Friday night, how would I be feeling Sunday night? I might well be in a full-blown panic. Yet here I was, ready to throw a whole night away numbing my mind. And that would likely roll into a full weekend of taking it easy.

I didn't need to be at the top of my accounting class to know that this was not a winning formula. I needed to buckle down with my studies, and I needed help if I wanted to get a decent return on my efforts. Friday night was the perfect time to look for it.

I gathered my accounting materials, threw them in my bag, and left the house—walking right past my brothers, already doing shots and grinning like hyenas in anticipation of the night to come. I made a beeline for the library.

I figured that anyone spending a Friday night in the library studying would be hardcore enough not only to thrive in class themselves, but to be able to teach me a thing or two. They'd probably even enjoy teaching me.

Often disciplined people are also caring people. And caring people are usually helpful people.

I walked through the library, and lo and behold, I spotted four kids from my class. The two Petes—Wiesenberger and Pasterell—and two girls—Joan Berkowitz and Edie Grossman.

"Hey!" I said, approaching the group. "What are you guys doing in the library on a Friday night?"

"We're hanging out here," they said. "We're having fun."

My frat brothers were hanging out and having fun. These kids were hanging out and having fun. But while one group was at an epic kegger, the other was at the library. It seemed pretty obvious which group was headed for bigger and better things in life.

"I really need to be a part of this group," I thought.

So I sat down with my classmates. They were each working on different things, but when I explained that I was having difficulty in accounting, they immediately showed a willingness to help me. They told me to take out my papers, and they began tutoring me.

I wasn't the quickest study, but I was teachable. Whether or not it was out of kindness, or amusement, or because it helped reinforce the concepts for them as well, this group took me under its wing. I began to hang out with them, and they tutored me whenever I needed it.

> Part of becoming the best is surrounding yourself with the best.

Later on that year, all of my fraternity brothers, friends, and basically everyone I knew were heading down to Fort Lauderdale for spring break. I didn't have the money to join them, but I never really doubted that I would come up with it. I just had to figure out how.

There was a club in Fort Lauderdale called The Button, which was the one of biggest spring break meccas in Florida in the late 1970s and early 1980s. The Button was famous for its wild college contests, which pitted students from different schools against each other in competitions including—on the modest end of the spectrum—basketball, beer pong, and wet T-shirt contests.

In case I couldn't make it down to The Button, I figured I'd bring The Button up to Syracuse. I convinced the most popular club and radio stations in town to cohost a giant, Buttonesque party one Saturday night at a local bar called Uncle Sam's. A family friend, Mo Berger, had some sway with local liquor distributors; he helped me persuade them to sponsor the bash with several premium labels and game prizes.

My right-hand man putting on the party was a Fiji brother a year younger than me, named Gary Gerome. Gary came up with the excellent idea of enlisting our fraternity pledges—with whom we had natural leverage—as worker bees.

We rounded up the pledges and told them that if they wanted to get into Fiji, it was in their best interest to help us throw this party. Then we drove them to other local colleges, like Le Moyne and St. Joseph's College of Nursing, and told them to fan out and invite everybody with a pulse. They were like little battalions, storming all the towns in the countryside.

We charged $2.94 to get in the door; then people could purchase three beers for $1.94 or two drinks for $2.94. We promoted it on the radio, in the streets, on campuses—wherever we went.

The night of the big party, almost 2,500 people showed up at Uncle Sam's. The line of cars stretched down the road as far as the eye could see. The club had a capacity of 1,500; we had to turn away a thousand people at the door!

The party ended up bringing in twice as much money as I'd hoped for. It was the first time I had put together an event on that level.

And the night really resonated at Syracuse; Gary threw the party after I graduated, and made some good coin. I'm proud to say he and I are still good friends, some 30 years later.

STILL ORANGE AFTER ALL THESE YEARS

I graduated from Syracuse in 1981, but I've kept my life entwined with the school.

In 2003, on the backs of precocious freshmen Carmelo Anthony and Gerry McNamara, Syracuse at long last won the NCAA Men's Basketball Championship. I knew we had to come up with a Steiner Sports product line that would commemorate the title for diehard fans and alumni like me. So we started Syracuse Steiner Sports Collectibles, and with the invaluable blessing of Hall of Fame coach Jim Boeheim, and the help of Athletic Director Daryl Gross, we were able to deconstruct the wood court in the Carrier Dome, where the team played its home games. (When I met Daryl, it was love at first sight; he has an energy and vision that only come along once in a while at a school.)

(continued)

(*continued*)

In addition to selling court pieces engraved with the team's record, and cutouts of the court mounted on plaques, we took some larger slabs and turned them into coffee tables and end tables. We even took tiny swaths and made them into cuff links. I have a pair of these myself; I wear them to add a little luck on days when I have big meetings.

The Syracuse basketball court line ended up being very successful, and we've expanded it with a similar product line from the University of North Carolina, and even one from the Knicks. Once, we even installed a large expanse of the 2007 Syracuse court as a brand new floor in a fan's office!

But the best part of Syracuse Steiner is that it's run largely by students at the university. Under Daryl's leadership, with assistance from my fellow alum and super sports agent David Falk and department director Michael Veley, among others, a few years ago we established an innovative partnership between our company and the school's department of Sport Management. (Once again, Coach Boeheim was a tremendous advocate for us.) Students work very closely with us in managing the division; they gain firsthand experience obtaining, marketing, and selling all of our Syracuse athletic memorabilia. It's the type of practical, real world education my mother would have appreciated. Not to mention John Dewey.

Every time I go up to Syracuse to give a lecture, or meet with fellow members of the school's Athletic Advisory Board, I'm thrilled to meet students who are getting their start in the industry through Steiner Sports. There's nothing like the feeling of pride you get from passing the torch to the next generation. I can't wait to see all the innovative products that they come up with.

YES OR YES

From the time I was 10 years old, I had been busting my ass doing a hundred different things at once. When I wasn't at some job, I was at school. There hadn't been any downtime. I never woke up in the morning wondering what I was going to do during the day, and I never went to sleep at night without being completely exhausted. But as the end of my senior year at Syracuse approached, I began to worry about what I was going to do next. All of a sudden I was staring at a blank calendar. It made me a little crazy.

Between my experience at the bagel factory, the hospital, and my various cafeteria jobs at camp, college, and the hospital, I had become passionate about the service industry. I loved everything about it—meeting and managing all sorts of folks, solving problems on the fly, working on my feet. Every day was a new adventure, and serving people was always very gratifying.

Perhaps my inclination at that time to work in the hospitality industry was inspired by the stories Cary told me about our grandfather, who had once owned some hotels. Or maybe hotels held a unique appeal for me, as places offering weary people a safe, clean, reliable place to stay—something I never had growing up. In any case, my dream job was to work for Hyatt Hotels.

Hyatt was the premier hospitality chain in the early 1980s. It was a growing company with a great reputation, an upscale clientele, and a high-profile management training program. I had always viewed myself as a manager, but I couldn't seem to get my foot in the door there.

So I applied to something like 200 jobs that were all over the map, literally and figuratively. I called everyone I could think of, sent my resume everywhere, went on interviews—and every prospect ended with a rejection of some kind. I didn't have a single job offer waiting for me when I finished college.

With no prospects in sight, my mother told me to go to Europe. She said she'd help me with the expenses.

"You've worked really hard your whole life," she said. "You deserve it."

She thought that was the classic thing to do, and plenty of my friends were going backpacking around Europe after graduation—but I couldn't do it. I couldn't take money from my mom; I knew she'd have to sacrifice too much for it. And I didn't want it enough to go into debt for it myself. Europe was out.

Graduation was getting closer and closer, and I still had nothing lined up. I felt like I was about to be hurled off a cliff.

I became so anxious that I developed shingles. Most people look back at their senior year of college as the last hurrah of youth, innocence, and freedom. For me, it was a time of stress and illness.

Then one day, I got a call from a career placement officer at the university. He knew I wanted to work for a hotel, and he told me about a new hospital in Baltimore that was opening up—it was going to be state-of-the-art, and was somewhat similar to a hotel. He thought I should reach out to them.

What the heck, I thought. My experience working at the hospital in high school had been exciting.

But before I contacted this hospital, I thought about the 200 rejections I had received. If I was rejected from so many jobs, there must have been hundreds, if not thousands, of others like me. I didn't see how, with those numbers, anyone could possibly stand out.

So I returned to my mother's famous question: *What Else?* What else could I do to separate myself from the hordes?

I found the name and address of the appropriate person at the hospital. I bought some nice stationery that I used to write a letter explaining that I had accounting experience, and cooking experience. I had worked in so many restaurants, I had done this and that, and I know I can be a help to you. Sincerely, Brandon Steiner.

Except the catch was, I wrote this all in red flair marker. And I printed my resume on green paper.

I don't know if I was trying to evoke the Christmas spirit in May or something, but I knew, at the very least, I wasn't going to get rejected for not standing out.

I put the papers in a manila envelope and dropped it in the mail.

One afternoon I was sitting around with an old camp friend, Frank Davis. Frank and I were on the verge of giving in and seeing if we couldn't somehow make it to Europe after all, when I got a phone call.

"Is this Brandon Steiner?" the man on the other end asked.

"Yes, it is," I told him.

"My name is Peter Zawackey," he said. "I run the dietary department at the GBMC. The Greater Baltimore Medical Center. You sent us your resume recently?"

"Yes . . . " I said, fairly cringing at the memory of flair marker.

"I just had to speak to the guy who's crazy enough to send a letter like this," he said. "You got to be kidding me. This is no way to write a cover letter."

I waited.

"...and I want to meet you."

So I drove down to meet Zawackey at the Greater Baltimore Medical Center, and we had a great interview. He hired me as an accountant, responsible for costing out medical supplies and overseeing patient admissions in the dietary department. He also asked me to oversee the inventory of the employee cafeteria where the doctors and nurses ate.

A month later, in August of 1981, I packed up my yellow Fiat 128, and moved my life to Baltimore. I had two $60 suits and $400 to my name. I didn't know a thing about Baltimore—including where I was going to be living and working.

My mother's friend Sara had a son named Joel who lived in Columbia, Maryland; my mom told me to call him. I could probably stay with him and his wife Susan for a while, until I could get on my feet. But the hospital had offered to put me up for two months, and being the proud guy I was, I didn't want to lean on my mother's friend. So I went with the hospital's accommodations.

When I got down to Baltimore I discovered that the hospital's accommodations were "unorthodox." They were going to put me up in a mobile home in a trailer park in Crofton, Maryland, 25 miles outside Baltimore.

I struggled from the very first night, out there in the wilderness and the darkness, with the quiet and strange sounds. I mean, I'm a Brooklynite from Ocean Parkway—I've been living in *Scarsdale* for years, and I'm still adjusting.

What made matters worse was that I was living in the trailer with another employee named Dale. Dale was not my ideal match for a roommate. He openly shared his hatred for Jews, blacks, all sorts of people. He was one of the most bigoted guys I've ever met. And everyone who worked at the hospital despised him.

Since I spent so much time monitoring the employee cafeteria, I got to know everyone from the surgery to the dish room. I really liked the hustle and bustle of food service. Also, I started organizing basketball games and various social events, becoming one of the most popular guys at the hospital. So Dale and I didn't exactly hit it off. Still, I was determined to make our situation work.

But even after three weeks of living there, I had difficulty finding the trailer park when I drove home at night. The road home was one of those back roads where you missed the entrance if you blinked. Here I was, a Brooklyn Jew, living with David Duke in a trailer park in the middle of nowhere—and I needed a map to find the place every night. I felt twisted up inside. I needed to get out of there.

I called my mother one night from the trailer park payphone.

"I can't take this," I said. "I gotta come home."

Again, my mom suggested that I call her friend's son Joel. But I was so stubborn; I still couldn't do it. I never wanted to rely on anyone else for anything. I felt that I had to do everything for myself.

Luckily, around that time, my boss at the hospital, Peter Zawackey, was getting divorced. (Lucky for me, of course—not him.) Peter knew about my situation, and he made me an offer.

"Look, now I have an extra bedroom in my house," he said. "Why don't you move in with me?"

Peter lived in Towson, which was like Preppyville, USA to me. I didn't think I'd feel comfortable living in that area, but it sure beat the trailer park. I took him up on the offer.

As luck would have it, a week after I moved in with him, Peter accepted a job in Saudi Arabia. There was a slew of new hotels and hospitals opening over there at the time, and that was a big move for someone in his position.

"I don't want to throw you out on the street," he said. "But you have three weeks to move."

In the meantime, he took everything. He left me with a couch, a lamp, a fork, a knife, a plate—that's it. I didn't even have the means to eat soup if I wanted it. I began to feel nostalgic for the days with Old Dale in the trailer park. And I had three weeks to find a new place.

So what did I do? I slipped into a bit of a funk, and I waited 20 days to do anything. Then my mother called me and asked me what my plan was.

"I don't know," I said. "I'll figure it out tomorrow."

"Why don't you call Joel," she said. "He wants to invite you for dinner at his house. I think he and Susan need a favor from you."

That shows how well my mother knew me, and how sharp she was. She knew that my pride would keep me from going over there for my own sake. But it was different if Joel and Susan ostensibly needed something from me. So I went over to have dinner with them. Joel had an offer of his own:

"We're going away for a couple of weeks, and we're afraid of leaving our son alone," Joel said. "Would you mind house-sitting for a couple of weeks, until we get back? In the meantime, you can look for your own place." Their son's name was Alan; he was 18.

I lived at Joel and Susan's for two weeks, took care of the house and the son, and had a great time.

When Joel and Susan came back, he told me I could stay longer.

"Alan is leaving to go to college soon," he said. "We'll have some extra room. Why don't you move into the bedroom in the basement?—you can have your own setup."

I felt like I might have been slow-rolled by Joel and my mother. Maybe the plan all along had been for me to stay there permanently. My ego was a little bruised. But I accepted the offer.

No one ever choked while swallowing their pride.

* * * * * * *

One day Joel and I were talking. "You work in this hospital," he said. "But what's the real story? What do you really want to do with your life?"

I told him that I had applied to all these hotel jobs and that I really wanted to work for Hyatt, but I hadn't gotten in anywhere.

"You're not going to believe this," he said. "But there's a Hyatt opening downtown soon, near the harbor. They're hiring."

I still didn't know my way around Baltimore too well, and I was nervous to go to the inner harbor by myself, so I put off looking into it. But Joel stayed on my case. He reminded me about the Hyatt three different times before I finally admitted that I didn't want to go down there alone. (I was getting better at this "accepting help" thing.) The next morning, Joel drove me there himself. It turned out to be the last day they were hiring.

I had three different interviews that day. I told them how much I enjoyed monitoring the hospital cafeteria, and how good I thought I was at it. In the end, I was offered the last food service management job available.

I had ended up working in a hospital in Baltimore partly because I hadn't been able to land a job with Hyatt. All of a sudden, I had one. In Baltimore.

From day one of that job, I worked my ass off.

My first post was a perfect transition from the hospital: managing the hotel's employee cafeteria and its staff of six. The hotel was run by almost 500 full-time workers, so the cafeteria got a lot of traffic. Hyatt was in the middle of an employees union battle at the time, and because management wanted to keep the staff as happy as possible, on occasion they let us create themed meals and special staff parties, I got to do a little bit of everything.

After four months of running a happy and bustling employee cafeteria, I was promoted to assistant manager of the hotel coffee shop, Cascades, during breakfast hours. I was told it was a promotion, but the first morning on the job, I had my doubts—which probably had to do with having to wake up at 5 a.m. every morning to open the shop. On my way over, in the dark, I used to pray that the staff would arrive on time; if someone was missing, I would be the one who had to do the dishes or bus the tables.

The job at Cascades proved to be one of the most difficult, most intense posts I've ever had in my life. I'd wake up at the crack of dawn to go down to the hotel, and there would already be 300 guests lined up, waiting to get in for breakfast when I got there. Every morning was an overflow crowd; it was *crazy* busy.

And I was responsible for making sure that everything went smoothly.

While my work at Cascades was invigorating, I dreaded having to wake up so early every morning. I could never get used to that.

But I couldn't quit. That was not part of my DNA. Rather, I had to find a way out.

"How can I get promoted?" I wondered. "How can I get to a higher position?"

What Else can I do for Hyatt?

"In my position, I can't bring more clientele into the hotel," I thought. "But is there another way I can make more money for the hotel?"

Then it hit me—increase the average check price.

Restaurants are always looking to grow the average amount of money their diners spend. Usually, they do this by pushing wine and other alcoholic beverages, and dessert. But those weren't options for a place that served so much breakfast; I was going to have to be more creative.

The impressive fresh-squeezed orange juice maker we had at Cascades gave me an idea.

I had just learned about the "Yes or Yes" theory at a sales seminar: Never ask a person a Yes or No question when it could be Yes or Yes instead.

I put a big display of oranges outside the entrance to the restaurant, and while guests were lined up to get in, I had a waitress ask each customer if they would like coffee or juice. Little room for a *no* in that question. As it happened, most people said "Both." Who doesn't want coffee and juice in the morning?

Pretty soon, the coffee or juice proposition became standard operating practice at all Hyatt coffee shops—along with the welcoming display of fresh oranges.

Simply thinking, "How can I run this place more efficiently?" might have sent me in a thousand different directions. But using the average check price as a guide—a measurement against which I could hold myself—showed me directly which areas I should focus on.

You can't manage what you can't measure.

At around the same time, Hyatt began computerizing its restaurant operations. Prior to this point, restaurants weren't computerized at all. When you ordered a dish off the menu, the waitress wrote it down on a check, and she had to run all the way into the kitchen and give it to the cook to read. Hyatt was the first restaurant chain to install a computer system whereby the waitress went to an electronic console and typed in an order, after which it was automatically printed out in the kitchen. This had never happened before. No one else had it. This machine was called the NCR-2160. The company, NCR, made cash registers, ATMs, bar code scanners, those sorts of machines.

I had absolutely no prior experience with computers myself. But the machine excited me. I took one look at that thing and knew it could accomplish a billion more *What Else's?* than I'd ever be able to imagine.

So I threw myself into learning how to use it. I made it my business to master it. Pretty soon there wasn't anything the NCR-2160 could do that I couldn't program.

Before I knew it, every manager in the hotel was coming up to me with questions about the NCR-2160.

"How do we use this thing?"

"I want to boost sales. How do I do it?"

I felt like I had the keys to the castle. Just taking the extra time to learn the machine—even though it wasn't one of my direct responsibilities—had made me into a huge asset for my colleagues.

It's crucial to stay current with technology. From the guy starting out in the mailroom, to the CEO in the corner office on the 50th floor, everyone has to be up to speed with the latest software and accessories. If you're not, someone else right behind you will be. And that person will provide the *What Else*—to your boss or your client or your customer—that you didn't.

On account of my record increase in breakfast revenues and my knowledge of the NCR-2160, I received yet another promotion. The management looked at the coffee shop as a training ground of sorts, and after just three months downstairs, I had proved that I was ready for the next level. Sales were lagging at Skylights, the restaurant on the top floor; they wanted me to take over as manager there.

Now I was working every *night*, running the hotel's most high-end restaurant, with its clientele of beautiful people, half-naked waitresses, extensive wine list, cocktail lounge, and view of all of Baltimore—lighting up the night sky below me.

The hotel was one of Hyatt's most successful locations up to that point. While Baltimore's inner harbor is one of the city's most thriving sections today, it was a desolate wasteland back then, and Hyatt was the first to plant a flag there. The chain really helped kick-start the resurgence of the harbor—and the city. It was a thrilling place to be, and I was right in the middle of the action.

I was lucky to come across people in Baltimore who wanted to help me out—Joel and Susan; the management team at the Hyatt, which was eager to teach me—but it was my dedication that turned those opportunities into good fortune.

In a few short months, I had come a long way from Dale and the trailer park.

As I said earlier, luck is the residue of hard work.

If you work hard and stay the course—and commit yourself one job at a time—you'll put yourself in a position to take advantage of opportunities that naturally arise. You'll also notice more opportunities than you did when you weren't committed—so while you might feel "lucky," you *made* these things happen. Opportunities are springing up around us all the time; the question is whether you're able to capitalize on them or not.

IF IT ISN'T EASY, IT ISN'T POSSIBLE

We had to have everyone out of Skylights by 2 a.m. to be able to clean up for the next day. But the mesmerizing view and décor and the intoxicating drinks and waitresses made it so that people never wanted to leave—and the status of the restaurant made kicking them out impossible. It was a problem.

I came up with a solution. Starting at about 1:30 a.m. most nights, I'd start playing offbeat disco music over the speakers in the cocktail lounge, and I'd ask some of the more attractive members of the staff to start dancing. The beat was just strong enough to get some diners to pay their checks immediately, so that they could join the dance party, and just grating enough to get the rest of them to pay their checks immediately so that they could leave. When the clock struck two, we'd cut the music, and with no other options, the dancers would file out.

One night, after we had started the disco music and I was making the rounds and cleaning up, a customer pulled me aside. He looked to be in his late thirties; I recognized him as a regular, though I had never spoken to him before. He introduced himself as JJ, explaining that he was in town as a hospitality consultant, advising a couple of the hotels that were getting set to open in the harbor.

"I'm in this restaurant practically every night," he told me. "I've seen how you manage the place, busting your ass. You're an interesting guy."

"Thank you," I said.

"I only work six months a year, myself," he said. "Would that interest you?"

"I think so," I said.

"Let me take you out to dinner," he said. "I can explain how. I have a set of truths to live by. I think you'll like them."

I happened to have the next night off. JJ picked me up and we drove to an Italian place. On the way over, this guy was just riffing on life. I barely understood half of what he was saying, but it sounded profound. I was very intrigued.

We got to the restaurant, sat down, and ordered.

"My truths are not exact," he said, "but if you follow them, they'll take you to a whole new level."

"Hold on," I said. I ran to get a pen and paper from the hostess, so I could write everything down.

"First truth," he began. "If it isn't *easy*, it isn't possible."

I wrote that down. He explained it a bit.

"Second truth," he continued. "You have the power to will things to be." I wrote that down. And on he went.

So began my collection of Steinerisms—a compilation of sayings that I try to live and work by, and which I try to expand to this day. JJ's theories seeded the collection.

The next night, he was back at Skylights. I went over to his table to say hello.

"I'm leaving Baltimore tomorrow," he said. "But I'll be back in a couple of months."

JJ'S *TRUTHS*

- *If it isn't easy, it isn't possible.*

     If driving to work seems to take too long and causes you stress every day, then you have to leave earlier, or find another way to get to work. To be successful, you need to be as efficient as possible in every area. When something in your life proves regularly complicated and taxing, you have to let it go.

- *You have the power to will things to be.*

     Capacity is a state of mind. If you really want something, you can get it, as long as you go all in. If you're not all in, you don't want it enough. You must be all in physically, mentally, spiritually and emotionally to reach your true capacity.

- *Be confident of your own value and worth by gaining consummate knowledge.*

     When people get upset about something, like not getting a raise, it has more to do with their own feelings of inadequacy than the thing that "happened" to them. But when you have total knowledge of yourself and your trade, when *you* know you know your stuff, there is a little that can fluster you.

- *It's not what you expect; it's what you inspect.*

     Accountability is crucial to success. That is to say: Game planning a project is important, but the plan is worthless if you don't constantly monitor its progress, and closely evaluate

(continued)

(continued)

it once the work is done, double-checking the details. Just as you're more likely to lose weight from a diet if you keep an eating log, so are you more likely to complete a task successfully if you carefully track its progress.

- *Steer people toward decisions. Don't push them.*

    Direct orders are forgotten as soon as they're completed. But if you steer someone toward reaching the desired decision for himself, the lesson will stay with him. It's the difference between telling someone to eat healthy, and showing them the benefits of healthy eating. Try and avoid telling people what to do. Inclusion breeds commitment and helps someone make a decision.

- *Know your place in the order of things.*

    Recognize that even though you may be working long hours, you might not be entitled to a raise if you're still a trainee at your company. Only after pinpointing your place in the order of things can you figure out how to move forward. A trainee should strive to move up the ladder, not to get a raise.

- *Win if you can, lose if you must, but always cheat.*

    Here, cheating means asking *What Else*, going the extra mile, gaining an edge. If you're trying to do a deal with someone, figure out what you can do for them beyond the parameters of the deal. Figure out how you can separate yourself.

- *You don't need to win every time to be a winner; you only need to win 51 percent of the time.*

    In business, you're not going to win every time. But you'll definitely lose more often if you don't take that risk, don't go for that new idea. In the end, being a winner means getting it right only a majority of the time. So don't be afraid to fail sometimes and don't let those failures overshadow your successes.

- *Don't snarl about customer requests. Embrace these requests.*

    We're living in a time when everyone wants to customize, personalize everything. You can say no to special requests, but before you do, try to be someone whose first instinct is to try to honor those requests. Don't let the word "no" become a reflex.

(continued)

(continued)

- *Acknowledge that you might be wrong, even when you know you're right.*

    Sometimes when you're trying to get someone to see your point, it pays to say "I may be 'wrong, but..." That will open up the other person to actually listening to your side of things, rather than dismissing your take out of hand—as they might think you're doing if you don't say that.

In the days and weeks that followed, the truths began to sink in. I could see them in action as I looked around at Skylights and watched my team and our customers. Or as was more often the case, I could see them missing in action. That gave me an idea.

On my next day off, I drove around the neighborhood and found an event space I could rent per night. Then I passed out fliers to the Hyatt staff. They said:

TIP$ ON TIP$

taught by restaurant consultant Brandon Steiner

HOW TO MAKE WORKING

IN THE

HOSPITALITY INDUSTRY

WORK FOR YOU!

for *servers* and *managers*

Steiner guarantees:

- a 33% increase in tip totals
- a 20% increase in sales
- or your money back! ($25)

I used my own experiences in food service—Sussex, the Hyatt, and so on—to breathe life into JJ's truths, and I wrapped it all up in a neat little presentation. I gave my little seminar six or so times; it was a small cult hit with food service employees in the area.

A couple of months later, I spotted JJ at Skylights one night. I was very excited to see him.

"I've been giving a talk based on the truths," I told him. "You should come by and hear it." I gave him a flier.

Sure enough, JJ showed up at my talk the next night. But after about 20 minutes, I noticed him leaving. I was crushed.

I saw him a couple of nights later, back at the restaurant.

"Why did you leave the other night?" I asked him.

"I've never seen someone explain the truths as effectively as you did," he said. "I felt overwhelmed."

I knew then that I really was an effective manager. I felt more confident than ever in my abilities to lead people.

To this day, I'm always looking for new people to look up to, mentors like JJ. Many of us—myself included—make the mistake of thinking we're done learning from others after we achieve some level of success or contentment. But it's crucial to constantly find new role models in your life, people who have been through things you're yet to experience: colleagues, business associates, authors, speakers, even celebrities. Though most of us aren't in school anymore, teachers are all around us.

GETTING THE RAISE, THEN THE JOB

I ended up staying in Baltimore and working at the Hyatt for two-and-a-half years; I did some work as a consultant to other hotels and restaurants for six months after that. I gained invaluable experience running those two hotel restaurants. It was the first time I had to put on a suit and tie to go to work, read profit and loss (P & L) statements, and manage a group of people. It was an exhausting, emotionally-taxing time during which I barely slept. But it was amazing. I was meeting so many people and consuming so much.

And what made it even better was that the hotel was a big success. The company initially had concerns about opening a hotel in an area undergoing transition, but it had had one of the best openings in the company's history, with around 90 percent occupancy. I performed so well that I even ended up doing some lecturing at the nearby Food and Beverage School at Essex Community College.

But my heart was still in New York, and I returned home in the fall of 1984. By this time, my mom was living in Rockaway, Queens, and I wasn't a big fan of the area. It's a beach community where one of the biggest pastimes was lying around in the sand all day, looking at the waves. I looked for a job as a restaurant manager, but I couldn't find anything; so I started doing some consulting work.

One day, I heard someone mention a new restaurant chain called Hard Rock Café. I had never heard of it, but apparently it was a hip restaurant that had already opened locations in London and Los Angeles. Now it was coming to New York; this location was going to be twice the size of the one in Los Angeles and 10 times that of London. It was definitely the next big thing

I *had* to get a job there.

I knew that thousands of people were going to be applying for jobs at the Hard Rock, but that didn't deter me. I wanted it badly; why would I let someone else get it without even trying?

I interviewed for an assistant general manager position at the midtown restaurant, with its signature façade: the front of a Cadillac bursting through the brick wall exterior. The management liked me well enough to call me back for a second interview, with the owner, Isaac Tigett.

I met Isaac at his apartment in the Sheffield, a swanky apartment building on 57th Street. I was wearing my best navy suit, and sporting a new, shorter haircut. I wanted to look like a pretty conservative guy. Even though I didn't have a job at the moment, my success at the Hyatt led me to consider myself a real manager—and I wanted to look the part.

Meanwhile, Isaac had long black hair and a beard, and he was wearing a black suit. I'd learn that he usually wore black. He was from Nashville, and always looked like he had just stepped out of the Grand Ole Opry.

"I have to find a way to stand out to this guy," I thought. "He's clearly not a typical restaurant owner." In addition to talking about my experience at the Hyatt, I told him the whole story about the bagels, the Button, anything I could think of that might resonate with him. I assumed he liked me, because the interview lasted well over an hour.

"You're a very interesting young man," Isaac said, finally wrapping it up. "I've really enjoyed this conversation."

I thought the job was in the bag.

Then as I was walking out, on the floor I saw, of all things, an NCR-2160—the machine from the Hyatt Hotel. I walked back in.

"Excuse me," I said, "but are you guys using the NCR-2160?"

The general manager, Eric Crisman—who had been in on part of the interview—popped his head in, as if on cue.

"What do you know about the 2160?" he said.

"I know a little bit about it," I said. "Hyatt basically designed the 2160 with NCR. It's their baby."

"NCR keeps trying to get us to use it, because we're going to be a multilocation operation," he said. "I'm really nervous about it. It's never been done before."

"I'm your guy," I said. "I know this thing."

Now, I *really* thought I had the job.

* * * * * * **

Long story short, I didn't get the job.

I was devastated. I was pissed off. I had had my eye on working for one of three companies: the Hard Rock, the Helmsley Hotel, or the Plaza. They were the best in their industries. And I didn't get a job with any of them.

With no better alternative, I accepted an offer to be the food and beverage director at a renovated Holiday Inn Crowne Plaza that was about to reopen in Danbury, Connecticut.

When I got there, I could immediately see that I not only knew more about the business than the current food and beverage director, but also more than the general manager. It wasn't good. I had just opened up a 250-seat restaurant in a brand-new upscale hotel in Baltimore, and now I was puttering around and living in a Holiday Inn Crowne Plaza in Danbury, Connecticut.

In 1984, Danbury was a relatively small, desolate town, and it seemed like it was always freezing outside. The hotel provided little solace; it was as cold and lonely as the town, except indoors. I felt like Jack Nicholson in *The Shining*. I was miserable. One weekend I went home, intending to go back to Connecticut on Monday morning just to quit.

"I'm done with this business," I said to my mother. "I'm finished."

"Why don't you go back to the Hard Rock?" she said. "See how they're doing. They just opened up the other day. I promise you, whenever people open up a new business, everything they thought they were going to do changes. Go and check."

I still wanted to work there. What did I have to lose? On my way up to Connecticut Monday morning, I stopped by the Hard Rock. I grabbed my only Cowboy hat out of the backseat, and asked if Isaac was there.

He wasn't, but Eric Crisman was. I was directed to his office.

"It's been a while," I said. "How's the 2160 treating you?"

Eric's eyebrows went up like a drawbridge.

"Oh my God, you wouldn't believe it," he said. "We've had so many files go down. No one knows what's going on."

"Sounds like you're having some problems," I said.

"Oh, we're having some problems."

"I wanted to remind you that I'm available for consulting," I told him. "If you need anything, give me a call."

Eric said he appreciated me stopping by. It was a quick visit; I was in and out.

I ended up spending three more days in Danbury helping out—after giving my notice. Then I returned to New York and moved back in with my mother.

I had been home for less than two hours and was still unpacking when the phone rang. It was a manager at the Hard Rock asking me to come in.

"We need your help with some problems," he said "Can you come in tomorrow morning?"

That's how fast your luck can change.

It was pouring rain when I got down there. I met with seven managers. They asked me some questions about the NCR-2160, just as I had expected, but their main problem was that the restaurant wasn't running very smoothly or efficiently at night—and they needed someone to turn that around.

During the day, a manager named Joyce Faiola ran the place. Joyce had been hired away from iconic New York restaurant Tavern on the Green. She ran a tight ship, and the Hard Rock needed someone to carry that atmosphere into the evenings after her shift was over.

The managers quizzed me on every possible dining contingency. As far as I was concerned, they couldn't ask me the questions fast enough. Hard Rock was one of the first truly large restaurants, with 250 to 300 seats; its business model happened to be right in my wheelhouse. At the Hyatt, I had essentially been a crisis manager for a high-end restaurant of that size, replete with new equipment and huge bursts of customers that were constantly streaming in. I had become adept at that type of staffing, level of traffic, and the kinds of crises that occur in that size establishment. Really, that was the only type of restaurant I knew. I saw so much room for improvement as I looked around the Hard Rock—so many areas where my experience would come in handy. My interviewers could see that I was high energy—that I knew what I was talking about, and would hit the ground running if they hired me.

This time, I got a job offer. It had taken three separate rounds of interviews, three different iterations of the same job search at the same restaurant, but I had stuck to it—and I was finally in.

The Hard Rock offered me a position as a manager—the job I had originally applied for weeks earlier. They said they'd pay me a salary of $25,000; the most I had ever made before was $22,500. All of the other managers were between 30 and 40 years old; I was 24. All things considered, it was a pretty attractive—and flattering—offer. But I felt I had some leverage, and I suspected they weren't aware of how much they actually needed me.

"I'm not interested in a manager job," I said. "Absolutely not."

It might have seemed as though Hard Rock had the leverage, as I had no other prospects and was living with my mother. But I *knew* I was going to be an asset to the place, and I was determined to act the part.

"You need somebody to come in here and really take charge," I said. "Let me be the assistant general manager, at $36,000. I'll run the whole place. Give me a two-month trial period, and if everything works out, I want my salary increased to $41,000. If it *doesn't* work after three months, you'll get rid of me, anyway."

Sometimes, it's wise to negotiate your first raise before you even get started!

If you're confident you're going to be an asset to your new team—and particularly if they want you for a high risk–high reward position—let them know just how valuable you're going to be while hammering out the starting salary. Put your worth where your mouth is by requesting more compensation after a certain period—in exchange for taking less up front. In most cases, it's a perfectly equitable arrangement—and what's more, it'll show them you mean business.

I had yet another reason for asking for more dough. Most of the managers at the Hard Rock were making $30,000 to $50,000. Since I was going to be younger than my staff, I needed to be the second-highest paid manager; there had to be something that made it clear to everyone that *I* was in charge.

In the end, they were convinced. The Hard Rock took me on as an assistant general manager—responsible for running the place at night, in charge of a staff of about 70.

ASKING FOR A RAISE

I say this often, but it always bears repeating: business is much more about people and relationships than it is about money. Any successful deal, product, or promotion has a team of caring, motivated people behind it. The money comes later.

The situation is no different when it comes to asking for a raise. Too many people approach their boss with a number in mind when they're looking for a higher level of compensation, thereby transforming the boss into the obstacle that stands between them and more money. They don't even realize it, but they're starting off in an adversarial situation—of their own creation.

You have to approach this situation as if you and your boss are a team. I was reminded of this recently when I spoke to Scoop Jardine, starting point guard for the Syracuse Orangemen. Scoop told me he wasn't satisfied with how much playing time Coach Jim Boeheim was giving him, and he wanted to ask his coach for more minutes.

But I suggested a different approach.

"Why don't you ask Coach how you can help the team more? Ask him where he thinks you can improve your game. Maybe there are things you haven't thought of, and he'll play you more if he sees you do them."

I told Scoop that it was important for him not to go into Jim's office and insinuate that he could manage the team better than Coach—which would be the inherent implication of protesting that

(continued)

(continued)

he wasn't getting enough playing time. He didn't want to take the coaching out of Coach's hands.

Instead, Scoop's question about where to improve his game would communicate to Jim both that he respected his ability to coach and that he was looking for a bigger role on the team. If he improved his game in the way Jim saw fit, Coach would be more likely to play him more. But if Scoop went in there only asking for minutes, Coach might conclude he was a little insubordinate, and not a real team player.

Hardly someone worth more minutes.

The same is true for an office dynamic. It's important not to try to manage your manager while asking for a raise. Instead, respect his or her right to manage; better still, engage that right.

It's also important to remember that too many employees request raises based on the work they've done already—that is, the contribution they think they've made to the bottom line thus far. But a raise is more about what you're going to do in the future. Ask your boss what more you can do, starting now, to help the business. Ask him where you can improve. Ask him about his general areas of concern for the entire company; you might have some ideas that can help.

This approach gives you more credibility to say: "If I do these things, do you think I might put myself in a position to earn more compensation?" You won't sound self-centered in requesting a raise. You'll come off like a team player. It's even effective to go into the meeting ready to delineate a few areas where you already know you can improve—and to pledge to do just that.

But make sure the time is right. Don't ask for a raise because something in your life external to the company requires it. If you have a mortgage payment due, or Christmas presents you need to buy—but your company is having a bad quarter—it's probably not a good time.

Finally, understand that asking for a raise is not a single conversation that occurs during a single meeting. It's a process that requires patience.

Again, it's all about your contribution to the team, not your personal stat line. If you find ways to increase your contribution, you'll likely earn more minutes (read: compensation).

My first night on the job at the Hard Rock, the problems that had been plaguing the restaurant were evident all around me.

Since the restaurant was extremely busy from open to close every night, some people who worked at the Hard Rock seemed to have the feeling that they didn't need to work all that diligently—that reputation alone would keep people coming. And with celebrities and rock stars constantly streaming in and out, some on staff took it for granted that the service was good. But in reality, it was poor and inefficient.

There were too many managers and waiters who thought they were part of a rock-and-roll consortium, running around in leather jackets every night, more focused on star "copulating" than cooking, serving food, and bussing tables. The staff was sloppy and disorganized. The restaurant was run so poorly that for the past couple of weeks, purses had regularly been snatched from the upstairs bar at night, and no one had done anything about it yet. It was a total circus. I had fought like hell for that job, and I was determined to make my mark. I couldn't get sucked into the orbits of the stars. I had a restaurant to run.

Don't get me wrong; I wasn't immune to the scene. Every night felt like an Oscar party. It wasn't unusual to see Elton John and Jackson Browne at a table, splitting an order of cheese fries and arguing about El Salvadorian politics, or to spot Jack Nicholson and Mick Jagger at a table in the back, sipping martinis and eyeing the "talent." I saw people like Wayne Gretzky and Lawrence Taylor; one night Willie Nelson got up and peed all over the bar.

Maybe it wasn't Studio 54, but it was a lot closer to that than a Denny's. It was hard not to get caught up in the scene. The Hard Rock was like an unending Mardi Gras: always a crush of people everywhere you looked—on the floor, at the tables, at the bar, at the door, by the restrooms. Music was blasting and cooks were yelling and waiters were flying around like armies of wasps.

And I was in the center of it all, trying to pull the right strings. Every day was a new adventure.

I was extremely focused from the first second of my first night. I made sure everyone did every little thing *to a tee*. No detail was small enough to avoid my utmost attention. I even made sure the cakes in the display behind the bar were always fresh.

One night I noticed that we were running low on silverware. Some people on staff suggested I just order another shipment, but I didn't feel that that was the appropriate way to address the issue. Problems wouldn't always be that easy to solve.

"How much you wanna bet there is silverware in the trash at this very moment?" I asked a group of waiters. "If we don't find any, I'll give you each ten bucks. But if we do, you guys pay me 10 dollars per utensil."

When I dumped out the trash bags, several forks and knives clanged onto the tile floor. The staff hadn't been throwing out silverware on purpose, but everyone was in such a hurry that they weren't paying enough attention to the individual tasks.

I worked on retraining the staff to see the bigger picture—to understand how each person's job and each duty they performed, no matter how small, was crucial to everyone else's performance (which in turn affected the bottom line and, more importantly to them, their tips). And just as every detail was important, so was every employee. In the winter, I brought soup to the bouncers who managed the line outside; in the summer, I brought them iced tea. If a dishwasher couldn't make it to work for some reason, I'd take over.

One of my strengths as a manager has always been my credibility with my employees. I don't consider myself separate from or above them. They know that if push were to come to shove, I'd get down in the proverbial muck with them in a heartbeat. And while establishing this dynamic was important to me at every managerial job I had in my career, I'd never had a more tangible way of proving it than I did one night at the Hard Rock.

I was doing my usual routine of running around and getting in everyone's business—you know, managing. I always tried to deliver my "orders" lightheartedly, like I was making a serious suggestion but joking around at the same time. If you can show your staff you have a sense of humor, it goes a long way. On this night, I noticed that the guy working the grill was being a little lackadaisical. A little sloppy.

"Be careful," I told him. "You're being a little lackadaisical."

He got a little ornery. I will spare you his more "expansive" language. Suffice it to say, his response ended with a simple directive.

"You take over," he said.

I didn't hesitate a second. Unbeknownst to the grill man, I had plenty of experience cooking on a grill from those summers at camp. I felt pretty confident.

As it happened, I ended up burning myself pretty badly. But I made some quality burgers. The staff noticed me working the grill, and I proved to everyone that there was nothing I wouldn't do. As the night drew to a close, I got on my knees with a flashlight and cleaned the grease off the floor.

You don't need to do other people's jobs as a manager. But your employees should know that you're willing to mop, bus, or get down on your knees with a flashlight to wipe up grease with them, should the need arise.

* * * * * * *

In addition to building credibility with the staff, I made it my business to establish credibility with the Hard Rock clientele.

As I indicated, in those days the restaurant was immensely popular with musicians and celebrities. There were always famous people there: Mick Jagger, Jeff Beck, Elton John, Jack Nicholson, Darryl Strawberry, Ron Darling, Keith Hernandez. (The Mets were there all the time.) While the rest of the staff was fawning all over these beautiful people, I made sure they got impeccable service, and didn't get taken advantage of if they were a little tipsy, or otherwise indisposed. I made sure they felt safe.

It didn't go unnoticed.

The stars saw how hard I worked. They came to rely on me. In that way, I developed real relationships with some of them.

I probably had more interaction with Keith Hernandez than anyone else. He stopped by most nights to meet up with friends. He frequently invited me to parties he was going to after dinner, or to go to a Mets game as his guest. But I wasn't as interested in being his friend as I was in being his favorite restaurant manager.

"How many times have I asked you to go to games?" Keith asked me one night at the restaurant.

"I wish I could go," I said. "But I need to be here."

He respected my answer.

I wasn't Keith's pal, but he saw me as a serious person.

Business goes up and business goes down; consistency over time is what equals credibility.

* * * * * * *

Every day, I was at the Hard Rock from about 3:00 in the afternoon to 5:00 in the morning. I managed nine people at the door and around 150 in the restaurant. Day or night, there was a line of 200 to 250 people waiting outside that wouldn't start to dwindle until 2 a.m.

I was on my game at the Hard Rock. It was some of the best managing I've ever done. I knew I was at the perfect place, at the perfect time. I couldn't wait to go to work every day, and I felt like I was coming down every time I left. Maybe that was why it wasn't unusual for me to call a meeting at 4 or 5 in the morning, when the rest of the staff was bleary-eyed and keeling over the tables, to go over what had happened the night before. There was always something I felt we could do better.

Unfortunately, I worked so intensely that I made myself sick. I was getting very little sleep and wasn't taking the time to eat right. I just wasn't taking care of myself; I was only taking care of the restaurant.

Your ability to succeed in any endeavor depends primarily on your state of mind. If you can summon the will to truly commit yourself, you can achieve almost anything. Occasionally, when you're in that zone, striving to operate at your highest levels, you get consumed. You forget to eat and shower. But that can be a good thing. No one makes money eating and showering.

I felt like I had the most exhilarating, rewarding job on the planet. But after a few months, I started to realize that no matter how far I rose at the Hard Rock, it would never be mine.

I could never truly be responsible for the Hard Rock's success. The ingredients for that were in place long before I arrived—the unique décor of authentic rock and roll memorabilia; the brand; the location; the celebrities who filled the place with electricity on a nightly basis. It was as if I had come in and flipped the switch of a powerful machine. I felt like I was running a family business, but wasn't a member of the family. No matter how much of myself I poured into the Hard Rock, it would never fill me up emotionally and spiritually.

So I started seeing the job as more of a learning experience. Every day on my way to work, I made believe that I was going to school. The restaurant was a giant classroom with teachers and lessons everywhere. I may not have an advanced degree, but the

Hard Rock was better than any business school. "What's bringing all these people here?" I asked myself. "What's inspiring them to wait two to three hours in line outside?"

* * * * * * *

I left the Hard Rock after working there about a year and three months. I heard that they increased the staff by about 30 percent to replace me. That was enormously flattering to hear—but it also made me realize that maybe I should have hired more staff. I couldn't believe I had tried to do so much by myself.

Managing at the Hard Rock probably took years off my life. But it was a very happy time for me—a priceless experience. I made so many friends and contacts. And because I was working so much, I didn't have time to spend the money I was making. I just salted it away, which would come in handy later on.

THE ONLY SPORTS BAR
IN NEW YORK

E ven though I was a sports fanatic my whole life, it took a dose of serendipity to steer me into the sports business.

One night while I was working at the Hard Rock, my girlfriend Nina came home with an announcement for me.

"There's a big sports bar opening downtown, in Tribeca," she said. "It's called The Sporting Club. You should go check it out."

In 1985, Tribeca (Manhattan's Triangle Below Canal Street) wasn't the fashionable, hip area it is today. It was a ghost town of abandoned cast-iron warehouses and factories, and decrepit, Colonial-looking brick buildings that had survived from the 1700s and 1800s.

The Sporting Club was located at 99 Hudson Street. Although Nobu and Tribeca Grill would open years later on that very block, the neighborhood was deserted at the time.

The restaurant had a big-screen TV, a scoreboard showing results of every game and race held that day, and pretty nice décor. Marble tables. Marble bar. White tablecloths. The service was very upscale. Many of the meals were cooked tableside, by waiters in smart, tailored uniforms. They were aiming to give their customers Vegas-style treatment.

The Sporting Club also had one of the first satellite dishes installed in New York City, but it seemed like no one there knew how to use the thing (trust me, it was no DirecTV). People would come from out of town just to see a specific game, and it often took 10 to 15 minutes for the staff to find the right broadcast. The owner was paying an arm and a leg for satellite service every month, and it was clear he was far from getting his money's worth.

The place was relatively empty. On any given day, there were 2,000 covers at the Hard Rock, while The Sporting Club seemed like it had about 5 to 10.

It was impossible not to see this cavernous, quiet restaurant's potential. A little voice in my head told me that what the Hard Rock was to music lovers, the Sporting Club could be to sports fanatics.

I introduced myself to the owner, Billy Rose, and we shot the bull for a bit. I told him I had some ideas for the restaurant. I knew I didn't need to describe them; I just needed to invite him.

"Why don't you visit me at the Hard Rock?" I asked him.

"What night is best?" Billy asked.

"Any night," I said. "It really won't matter."

He came on a Tuesday, which was perfect. Normally, Tuesday was a pretty quiet night all over the city. It was anything but that at The Hard Rock. The place was bumping.

I gave Billy a tour and we sat down for a drink.

"Look at this place," I said, sweeping the room with my arm. "Why can't we do this with the Sporting Club?"

"I don't know," he said. "You think that's possible?"

"Definitely," I said. "Besides, I can't watch any games working here."

I felt confident that I had acquired the skills and know-how to turn around the Sporting Club. And since it didn't have much of a personality, I knew I could put my own mark on it. I couldn't wait.

My work at the Hard Rock, and my eagerness to give it up to work for his empty restaurant impressed Billy sufficiently. He offered to double my salary, make me the general manager; and he promised me a percentage of profits.

It was a done deal.

Billy's vision had been to model his place after The 21 Club, a famous restaurant, bar, and lounge in midtown that had originally opened in 1922 as a speakeasy. Decorated with antique toys and sports memorabilia, it's been featured in countless movies and TV shows, and it's been a go-to hangout for celebrities, politicians, and even gangsters. Jeans were not permitted. Men had to wear jackets and ties. It was as ritzy and prestigious as New York City got, and the closest you could get to Las Vegas glamour in New York.

But the Sporting Club fell far short of The 21 Club. Billy had neglected the intangibles that made The 21 Club famous—the star-studded clientele, the Prohibition history, the overall reputation and buzz. He had a shell without the filling. It was a 12 at best; maybe a 13.

The place had been open for about a month, but most nights, only a few people came in.

One night I invited Keith Hernandez and his crew to the Sporting Club. After he sat down, Keith looked around at the empty tables, and then he looked back at me.

"Are you crazy?" he asked, bewildered by my decision. "You left the Hard Rock for *this?*"

But all I could see was potential. At the time, there were only two veritable sports bars in the country where you could go to watch a non-local game on satellite or closed-circuit television: Bobby V's in Stamford, Connecticut, and Ultimate, in Chicago. There was more than enough room in New York City for such a place.

I went to work.

My first order of business was learning how to properly operate the satellite dish.

It's nice to have assets. But if you're not properly utilizing them, they're nothing but liabilities.

I brought in a treasure trove of sports memorabilia and a slew of additional televisions to liven the place up. I reinvented the menu. Basically, I turned the place into the basement I never had as a kid—albeit a bit more upscale. I retrained the entire staff.

I worked like a dog. I didn't have set hours. When I woke up in the morning, I went to work. And I stayed until 2 a.m. Five months straight, without a day off.

Most importantly, I brought the buzz.

The Hard Rock taught me many, many things—but the one thing that really stood out was that celebrities attract people.

STARS AND BARS

On nights when business was slow I invited celebrities I knew from the Hard Rock to come and tend bar. Part of the proceeds always went to charity; liquor and soda companies helped me promote the appearances. Sometimes I even got a little radio time. There were

(continued)

(continued)

nights when you could go to the Sporting Club to see a big football game or boxing match, and the likes of Carl Banks, Wayne Gretzky, Jerry Cooney, Mark Gastineau, or Walt Frazier would be behind the bar, mixing drinks. We gave them a little training when they got there, but they pretty much winged it. When Wayne Gretzky makes you a martini, it tastes delicious no matter what the heck's in it.

Creating celebrity bartender nights was one of the biggest initiatives I undertook at the Sporting Club. It was a page straight out of my mom's playbook, a lesson on bringing in customers on usually-slow nights. You'd be surprised how much room there is to turn your worst business days into some of your best. My mom used to promote two-for-one deals on wash and sets at the salon on her slow nights. At the Sporting Club, I wrangled up celebrity bartenders.

The Celebrity Bartender Nights were a huge success, and they began to bring to the Sporting Club the kind of traffic Billy had envisioned when he opened the place. Soon, they naturally evolved into our Fight Nights.

Boxing was huge in the 1980s. It was the last golden age for the sport, with icons like Sugar Ray Leonard, Roberto Duran, and Mike Tyson enjoying their primes. There were great fights all the time, and everyone wanted to watch them.

The problem was that hardly anyone had cable back then, let alone HBO or Showtime. And forget pay-per-view. So most people just couldn't watch boxing at home. Bars, restaurants, and movie theaters bought the rights to big fights on closed-circuit television—or via satellite—and people came to watch them. At the Sporting Club, there were even a lot of athletes and celebrities who regularly came in to watch boxing.

I turned this standard practice into a celebrated event at the Sporting Club. I paid some of the athletes and celebrities—who usually came in to watch the fights *anyway*—to come for my special Fight Night parties, and we promoted those appearances ahead of time. The place would get totally packed.

We really did it right. We had great food and liquor. We even had ring girls. It was a huge party, like at the Hard Rock, but for sports fans. That was the first time I really began to *work* with athletes and celebs—hiring them for our Fight Nights. We regularly drew names like Mickey Mantle, Charles Oakley, Lawrence Taylor, Dan Marino, Alex Trebek, and Dustin Hoffman. It wouldn't be unusual to have 10 to 20 stars at a Fight Night.

We were basically the first true sports bar in the country. Sure, there were bars that featured sports on TV, but we were the first to *focus* on sports. The Sporting Club was the place to be—and my Rolodex grew fatter and fatter.

One night we hosted a huge charity event where we inducted three athletes into the newly created Sporting Club Wall of Fame: Knicks legend Walt Frazier; Rangers legend Rod Gilbert; and Floyd Patterson, former heavyweight champion of the world. A cadre of stars showed up, including sizable contingents of Yankees and Mets players.

I couldn't believe it. New York City's major leaguers—coming to an event *I* created!

My mom had visited the Sporting Club when I first started there and had seen how empty it was. On this night, four months later, she had to fight through a long line and a crush of people inside just to reach me.

I remember seeing her big hair weaving through the crowd, like a periscope above the surface of the water. When her colorful face appeared, it revealed a shining smile.

She gave me a big hug.

"Do you realize what you've done here?" she said, beaming. "I think you got it. I think you're ready for big things."

WAITING TO BE STRUCK BY LIGHTNING

A couple of years ago, I saw the documentary *Joan Rivers: A Peace of Work*, which chronicles the life and career of the fearless—and Brooklyn-raised—comedienne. In the film, discussing Joan's unbelievable resilience, her friend Larry Thompson says, "You can't get hit by lightning if you're not standing out in the rain. Nobody can stand in the rain longer than Joan Rivers."

This quote resonated with me because people are always asking me: "How did you get started?" But I can't single out any *one* moment as the point where I got started. The answer is as long as this book! In other words, my success was more about standing in the rain and capitalizing on the opportunities—the lightning bolts—when they came along, even when they weren't quite what I envisioned.

But for those who want something slightly more specific—well, let's just say this chapter comprises some of the more formative rainstorms I stood in as my career really began to take shape.

MAKING CONNECTIONS

After working at the Sporting Club for about 14 months, Billy and I began to get under each other's skin a bit. I felt he was a little too lax as an owner—that he wasn't sufficiently detail-oriented to maximize the restaurant's potential. Looking back, I'm sure Billy thought I was a little too intense. I eventually left, but in the end, it was a pretty amicable split.

My leaving the Sporting Club was a more important turning point for me than I realized at the time. From my time managing the restaurants at the Hyatt in Baltimore, through the Holiday Inn in Danbury, the Hard Rock, and most recently the Sporting Club, I had more or less been working over 12 hours a day, seven days a week, for almost four years. And it wasn't like I had been sitting at a desk. It was four years of loud music, smoke, junk food, tending to movie stars and athletes and drunks, and all the rest of it. I was burned out. Physically and emotionally. I had trouble sleeping. I was only 26 at the time, but I felt like I was 100.

At the tail end of my time at the Sporting Club, Billy had recommended to me a therapist named Rita Sperling. I began seeing her twice a week. The year or so I spent in therapy with Rita was a tremendous step for me. She helped me recognize that I was still angry and confused by my childhood. (Initially she couldn't quite believe that the stories of my childhood weren't exaggerated, so my mother even came with me for a few sessions, to corroborate them.) Rita helped me come to terms with some of the issues I had from that period. For a long time, I had needed to take my foot off the gas; now, with some help, I was finally able to slow down a bit. I changed my attitude for the better; I started to behave more consistently with my family and friends, and to think seriously about where I was and where I was going.

A positive attitude opens up doors you don't even know are there, and this time period was a good example of that. Right around the time I started counseling, a friend of mine introduced me to a man named Peter DuPre.

Peter was a co-owner of the Amsterdam Restaurant—appropriately located on 81st Street and Amsterdam Avenue—which specialized in rotisserie chicken. He and his partners were going to open a new Amsterdam, in West Soho. Familiar with my prior bar and restaurant experience, Peter asked me to spearhead the marketing and launch of this new location.

After leaving the Sporting Club, I had started looking for a job that would be less taxing, with a more manageable work schedule, so I was more than happy to accept Peter's offer. The job paid less than my previous managing gigs, but it was something I knew I'd be good at—and that wouldn't wear me out. It turned out to be just what the doctor ordered. For a couple of months, I created and executed various promotions and advertisements for the new Amsterdam—and for the most part, I was able to do it all at my own pace.

Shortly after the new Amsterdam opened, that restaurant and the original sister location were acquired by the Astor Group—a franchisor of Blimpie's sub shops outside New York City, that also co-owned with Yankees great Dave Winfield the Border Café, a joint that served Southwestern cuisine. Based on the success of the Amsterdam opening, the Astor Group asked me to take a position working out of their corporate office, promoting their full slate of restaurants.

Once again, I was thrilled to accept the offer. I knew there was only so far I could go at the Astor Group—I'd never be asked to be a partner—but it was a great opportunity nonetheless. For the first time in my entire life, I worked normal hours in a normal office. Still in therapy with Rita, I finally had the time and presence of mind to fully recharge my batteries. It was a real blessing. I chilled out (as much as I could) and just enjoyed life in New York City for a couple of years.

My favorite thing about those days was my lunch hour. Naturally, The Astor office was located near Astor Place, at 7th Street and Third Avenue. Almost every day during lunch, I went over to the 14th Street Y, to play in a pick-up basketball game that often included Peter Vecsey, syndicated NBA columnist for the *New York Post*; former editor of the *Post*'s famous Page 6 gossip section, Richard Johnson; and NBA announcer Mike Breen. We were also occasionally joined by a guy named Rock, who coached Samuel Tilden High School in Brooklyn, and who one time cracked my head open when I drove in the lane against him. I always made sure to keep in touch with the people I met in those days. I was a natural networker, asking everyone for their business card, or phone number, constantly adding to the Rolodex.

Toward the end of my time working at the Astor Group, the partners decided to open another Border Café. Chuck Leonis, the Astor partner who was leading the effort, asked me to direct public relations (PR) and promotion for the new place.

As it turned out their partner, Dave Winfield, was a real "all-in" guy. He was very invested in the business. Dave wasn't satisfied just to have his name on the corporate documents; he very much cared about the details of the operation. So while working to set up the new Border Café, I developed a friendship with the baseball great—one that I'm thrilled to say continues to this day.

It's strange to think that, having met all these other athletes through the Hard Rock and Sporting Club, I would meet Dave Winfield—in the prime of his Yankee career—through a completely different channel. Looking back, it's hard not to see fate at play, gently pushing me toward a particular career path. But at the time, it just seemed like another little reward for some hard work.

Around the same time, a restaurateur named Bill Liederman reached out to me. He was partnering with Mickey Mantle to open a sports-themed bar and grill on Central Park West. Bill knew about my work with the Astor restaurants, and he offered me a small piece of Mickey Mantle's, if I would leave the Astor Group to come and manage all marketing for the new restaurant.

I declined Bill's offer. I didn't think the place would be a success.

The restaurant opened in 1988 and quickly established itself as one of the most popular restaurants in New York.

* * * * * * **

Although I did not accept Bill's offer, over the years he hired me as a consultant for several events and promotions at the restaurant. Getting to know Mickey Mantle was a dream come true for me. And since I met him through Bill, who told him I was a good guy, whom he could trust, Mickey was great to me from the get-go.

The right introduction can go a long way.

(In fact, down the road, Mickey was instrumental in my successfully signing crucial deals with Yogi Berra and Phil Rizzuto.)

THE '86 GIANTS

One of the regulars when I worked at the Hard Rock was a guy named Lee Lipton. Lee was an important figure in the garment industry, and he used to come into the restaurant with fashion models and New York Mets, Giants, and other athletes. When I left the Hard Rock for the Sporting Club, Lee took it upon himself to introduce me to some friends of his whom he thought could be of some assistance to me.

"I don't know what you're getting into here, with a theme bar in the middle of nowhere," he said. "But I know some guys who might be able to help you out."

Lee introduced me to Hank Mackin (nicknamed H), who ran a stuffed toy company, and Kevin Heller, a jewelry maker and classic guy-who-knows-everyone-everywhere. Kevin's brother was a lawyer in Florida, with strong ties to the University of Miami's football team; through him, Kevin knew a slew of pro athletes who had passed through that program. Still more athletes sought him for custom-made jewelry. The guy had a lot of connections. It was through H and Kevin that I first got to meet several big athletes, including Lawrence Taylor, Carl Banks, Darryl Strawberry, Ron Darling, Jim Burt and Herschel Walker. They often hung out together and would invite me out as well.

The year 1986 was a spectacular stretch for New York sports. After the Mets won the World Series in historically dramatic fashion, the New York Football Giants steamrolled their own competition, to the tune of a 14-2 record. They were all set to host the Redskins in the NFC Championship Game in January 1987.

Peter DuPre came up big-time once again. The morning of the NFC Championship, Peter called to tell me he had four tickets to the game and asked if I wanted them. Tickets to that game were impossible to get, and these seats were on the 40-yard line.

I called H and Kevin; the three of us went with another friend of Kevin's, Danny Stubbs, a standout defensive end at Miami who was drafted by the 49ers a year later and went on to play for five different teams in the NFL.

As the Giants were putting the finishing touches on their 17-0 victory over Washington, Kevin turned to me and promised he was going to pay me back for the tickets—by taking me to Super Bowl XXI, at the Rose Bowl in Pasadena. (Because of the rivalry between the Giants and the Redskins, the NFC Championship tickets were more difficult to come by than Super Bowl tickets that year. While Kevin's player connections hadn't been enough to score tickets for the NFC title game, they readily afforded him Super Bowl tickets.)

The trip out west was fantastic. We all flew out together. On the strength of Kevin's connections, it felt like we were royalty being shown around LA. Everywhere we went, we seemed to know everyone. It seemed like there were Hall of Fame athletes and big-time celebrities spilling off of every street corner. The day before the big game, we even went to the players' hotel, to visit Giants' running back Joe Morris. Joe was a friend from our shared time at Syracuse.

Joe was rooming there with Giants tight end Zeke Mowatt. While we were hanging out in their room, I noticed a stack of messages on the desk: the messages were for calls from Johnny Carson, David Letterman—it seemed like every television show and news outlet was trying to get a hold of them.

I had an epiphany of sorts.

"Joe," I said, leafing through the message slips. "Who is helping you with all this?"

"No one, really," he said.

"I want to help you with this when you get back to New York," I said.

Sure enough, Joe Morris was my first ostensible client. He was quickly followed by Keith Hernandez, Darryl Strawberry, and David Cone of the Mets, and Lawrence Taylor and Carl Banks of the Giants.

I had effectively started my own celebrity marketing and event agency. I incorporated it as Steiner Associates. It was 1987.

MEETING MARA

While working for the Astor Group, I decided to throw a fund-raiser for my old camp, Camp Sussex, which was for underprivileged kids. I had spent some great summers there, first as a camper, and then as an employee. I was grateful for my time there; every year since my last summer at camp I had found a way to raise money for it.

We held the fund-raiser at the Amsterdam restaurant in West Soho. I promoted it everywhere I could, but I never could have imagined how far word would travel.

As I was watching the people streaming into the event, in walked someone I didn't expect to see: Mara Wagner, my first love, whom I met at camp when I was 17.

Mara had grown up in Five Towns, Long Island, an area much more affluent than my own. Her parents had sent her to Camp Sussex so that she would get to know kids from more modest backgrounds. They wanted her to get to know both sides of the world, as it were. Unfortunately, she got to know me.

But I hadn't seen her for eight years.

Then there she was that night at the Amsterdam. She took the wind right out of me. She looked fantastic.

I was speechless, but fortunately, Mara came up to me and broke the ice. We talked for a while, and the whole time I knew I was in trouble. She was really pretty and very smart, and she had these great blue eyes.

Even though we had parted ways when we both went to college, I had never forgotten about Mara. It was Mara who first got me to think seriously about college. She had had a huge impact on my entire view of the world; she made me see the bigger picture. She was the love of my life.

Mara went to Wharton for undergrad, and even though we saw each other only two times in college, I made sure to check up on her through mutual friends now and then. She was always in the back of my mind, but I never really thought that we would reconnect after all those years. Now she was a semester away from getting a master's in finance from the University of Chicago.

We went out to dinner a few nights after the fund-raiser. Seeing the woman she had become, I was even more thunderstruck than before.

Mara was interested in hearing all about what I had been doing, and she had really good insights about it all. We began dating, even though she was still living in the Windy City.

Amazingly, when Mara completed her degree and moved to Manhattan, she settled into an apartment on the Lower East Side—mere blocks from the Astor Group office. I had been living on the Upper West Side, and it was difficult not to read the circumstances as some kind of sign from above. Not long after, Mara graciously let me move in with her.

Mara is the most secure, sensible person I know. With me in mid-air and Mara's feet planted firmly on the ground, we achieved a nice equilibrium. We complemented each other very well and made a great team.

In 1988, we got married—it's 23 years and counting.

ONE THING LEADS TO ANOTHER

During my time with the Astor Group, I produced a handful of fight nights on the side—like the ones I hosted when I worked at the Sporting Club. Through my work there, I had met a man named Donald Lipeles, who currently runs Madison Sports Management, a marketing agency. In those days, Don owned a satellite TV company; he would accompany me when I needed to bring certain television equipment to a restaurant.

Don and I put on some very large fight nights at discotheques around the city including 4D and Club 1018. We charged as much as $250 and even $500 a head for these premium parties, and people still lined up around the block to get in. We drew thousands of paying customers to our bigger events.

These events attracted corporate types who wanted to show their clients a good time. In addition to the big screens we had hooked up to the satellite feed, we had the ring girls and everything; it was just like you were there in person.

And just as they had at the Sporting Club, celebs showed up. Dustin Hoffman, Alex Trebek, Lawrence Taylor, Charles Oakley, Dan Marino, Ottis Anderson, Mark Jackson—all of them could practically have been called regulars. I'll never forget that at one of these fight nights, Eddie Fischer sang the national anthem!

Of course, I had long had designs on opening a sports bar of my very own. I had a vision. It was essentially going to be like the ESPN Zone—except a decade before the ESPN Zone existed. At one point I had raised about $300,000 from everyone and their mother—and my mother—and I looked at a lot of spaces. But it just didn't come together.

Then, in 1989, Don Lipeles called me with an offer. He told me that he and a few associates were going to start their own small marketing agency. The group was composed of Don, who was going to handle player marketing and autograph signing with Mead Chasky, who was tight with all of the '86 Mets; and David Lin, a lawyer who represented several Yankees. Don asked me to come on to spearhead the food service side.

"We're going to be like a mini-IMG," Don told me, referring to the sports marketing and media behemoth.

That night, I talked things over with Mara. In order to accept Don's offer, I'd have to give up my steady job at the Astor Group. But Mara agreed that the invitation sounded like a great opportunity, and it was worth the sacrifice. Besides, I think she was probably relieved that joining this new firm would put an end to my dream of opening my own enormously risky sports bar. So that Monday morning, rather than train down to the East Village, I headed to midtown, and reported for work at my new office, at 645 Madison Avenue, 60th Street in Manhattan.

No sooner did I reach the 10th floor and walk in the door, however, than Don pulled me into his office. He proceeded to explain that he and the other guys had decided that they didn't need me to be a partner, after all. I was free to keep my one-room office, inside their two-floor space, so long as I rented it from them. But I was no longer going to be part of their new company.

I felt humiliated. I can't say it was as bad as that time in fifth grade when Mr. Kerper gave me money to buy new clothes, but it was in that ballpark of feeling. Still, I had no choice but to take Don up on the office rental; for at least a month, I had nowhere else to go.

A few months later, Don and David and the rest of them determined that they couldn't make their arrangement work, and they all moved out of the office! Now I was working in a ghost office.

ON MY OWN

I did anything I could to stay afloat. I went back to hosting events at venues around the city: guest bartender nights tying together celebrities, charities, and liquor companies; fight nights; other celebrity events, like golf outings. All sorts of marketing campaigns for all sorts of bars and restaurants.

I sold fight night packages to restaurants like Mickey Mantle's and Tavern on the Green. I'd sell them the satellite broadcast, celebrity clientele, and the other necessary ingredients for a great fight night, and they'd sell tickets. I sold some packages to corporations that held fight nights in their conference rooms for their employees and associates. I built up a steady little business for myself. I even ended up helping to open a few bars as far away as Miami. All the while, it was becoming more and more apparent that sports moved people as much as celebrities did.

Still, as time marched on, more and more people were signing up for cable subscriptions and getting access to pay-per-view at home. I knew that soon they weren't going to need to leave their homes to watch boxing, or any other sport. The business model of organizing promotions and events around premium sports broadcasts wasn't going to last much longer.

The final nail in the coffin came in 1991, when Mike Tyson was convicted of rape. He had been scheduled to fight Evander Holyfield for the heavyweight championship in November of that year; I had lined up big fight events at several bars. It was going to be my biggest payday yet, and when Tyson got locked up, it became a crippling loss. I was going to have to find other ways to make my business work.

Before the end of the fight night era, however, I got a phone call from my friend Michael Ritz. And no matter what you call it—fate, luck, coincidence—that phone call was a product of years of hard work creating sports events at bars.

Michael worked at the Howard Marlboro Group, with a man named Don Raskin. Currently a senior partner at Manhattan Media Ensemble, at that time, Don ran the promotional department of HMG. Cutty Sark Scotch Whiskey had just hired the firm to create a promotional campaign; Michael recommended to Don that they farm out the work to me. At first Don was reluctant to give away any business, but Michael convinced him that I had a unique skill set to bring to the account, based on my experience working with celebrities to market restaurants and bars.

After all, in reality, I didn't have to be a competitor. If I helped create a great campaign for Cutty Sark, it would only reflect well on HMG, strengthening the trust between the two companies. (I'd be the *What Else* HMG could provide to Cutty.)

Needless to say, no sooner did Don call me with the parameters of the project than my mind started racing, dreaming up possible events for the whiskey brand.

I had recently done some promotions with bars that had Pop A Shot arcade games. In these games, you take as many free throw–type shots as you can in one minute, while arcade lights flash and your score is recorded on an LCD display.

I had always been a fan of Rick Barry. A former ABA and NBA superstar, Rick wasn't just one of the best free throw shooters in history; with his unorthodox, underhand, two-hand technique, he was the most iconic and recognizable free throw shooter of all time.

Even though he was working as an NBA broadcaster for TBS, Rick was being underutilized commercially. It was a perfect formula; with his reputation as a legendary free throw shooter, and known national TV presence—along with his limited commercial exposure—Rick was the perfect athlete around whom Cutty Sark could run a dynamic promotional campaign.

I envisioned a nationwide series of sports bar appearances that would coincide with Rick's schedule broadcasting NBA games around the country for TBS. At each stop, Rick would be the guest of honor at a popular bar with a Pop A Shot; a contest winner would face off against him in a competition. And, schedule permitting, a local NBA star—from past or present—could be paid to show up as well. Cutty Sark would sponsor it all, paying for Rick—and anyone else—as well as providing free booze and promotion of the bar and event. In turn, Cutty Sark's name would be indelibly linked to one of the best events of the year in that city.

The Marlboro Group loved the idea and agreed to support the events. I began to book the flights, appearances, and parties. I had just hired my first intern, George Ameer; he was tremendously helpful in pulling off that project. (George works for the PGA Tour now, as a manager for International Television.)

The campaign went on for the good part of a year, and covered New York, Miami, Chicago, Los Angeles, and Boston. It was a big success. In each city, the bar at which we hosted the Pop A Shot party was packed, and the event garnered significant attention on local TV. Rick was always immensely personable and the shooting contest itself was inevitably dramatic, an exclamation point on the night. The bartenders served Cutty Collins and Cutty Rickey drinks, and the brand got great exposure.

In addition, I'd call local liquor stores and arrange lunches with Rick for their owners and the local distributors. Even those lunches were packed in most cities. The whole tour drove home for me the power with which athletes and media exposure move customers.

MAKING THE MARKET

Combined with my star-studded restaurant experience, the Rick Barry promotion confirmed my sense that in the sports business world, there was a need for someone to serve as a liaison between athletes and Madison Avenue. I wanted to be that guy. But I wasn't completely sure how to go about it, how to put the pieces together. Then Kevin Heller opened up a door for me, yet again. (You can never have enough friends.)

Kevin introduced me to Marty Blackman. A former star ad executive, Marty was the brains behind the famous Mean Joe Greene Coke commercial, and was one of the first brokers to match up celebs and athletes with companies for promotional purposes. He was an original sports marketing guru. Kevin introduced us, and I got to pick Marty's brain.

Marty knew from his own experience that while a lot of businesses wanted to book athletes for appearances and promotions, the process was complicated and difficult. Some athletes received many requests, but were too expensive. Others would have been happy to do it, but were difficult to get to. There were guys who were easy to work with and guys who were very difficult. Companies were having a tough time navigating it all.

Marty explained that there were a lot of people representing players, but nobody representing companies—and they were the ones who really needed the help. He suggested that there was an opening for someone—namely, me—to help companies figure out ways to pair with players as a way to drive sales.

If a company was going to have a golf outing, or a sales conference, I could match them up with an athlete. Ideally, if it was a good connection, the athlete would inspire the participants and generally make the event more productive. And since it was all ancillary income for the athletes, they wouldn't come too expensive. Everybody wins.

The first thing I had to do was get a stable of athletes I could pitch. Thanks to Kevin's network, I had a few guys on board already, but not enough to get a serious business going. Fortunately, Rick Barry had many athlete connections, through his TV and charity golf event work, that he offered to share with me.

Tapping the money I had saved from the Sid Loberfeld–Pepsi settlement in high school, I signed a lease for a 200-square-foot office share that was part of a 5,000-square-foot space. My first intern, George, was succeeded by an intern named Tiny Gerome—younger brother of my old frat buddy Gary Gerome. Tiny was a hard worker and an invaluable asset, despite making it fairly clear that he thought I was a lunatic. Together, we sent out letters to as many athletes as I could think of, asking each one to become a part of a sports speakers bureau. In those days, nobody had cell phones or e-mail. All I had was addresses for these guys, at their pro sports team facilities. In most cases, no one even knew how to get in touch with their agents.

After three straight days of printing, stuffing, and sending letters, speakers bureau invitations had gone out to hundreds and hundreds of athletes—all over the country.

A lot of rejection letters flowed in, but there were also a fair amount of yeses. Most of those explained that they had nothing to lose.

TWO ACTUAL REJECTION LETTERS

MIAMI DOLPHINS

JOE ROBBIE STADIUM

MIAMI, FLORIDA 33056

October 26, 1989

Brandon Steiner

Steiner Associates

645 Madison Avenue

New York, NY 10022

Dear Mr. Steiner:

Thank you for your letter. I appreciate your asking however at the present time I would not be interested in being included in your speakers bureau brochure for this year.

Best wishes.

> Sincerely,
> Don F. Shula
> Head Coach &
> Vice President

UNIVERSITY OF NORTH CAROLINA

CHAPEL HILL, NC 27514

November 16, 1989

Mr. Brandon Steiner

Steiner Associates

645 Madison Avenue

New York, NY 10022

Dear Mr. Steiner:

Thank you for your recent invitation to be a part of Steiner Associates Speakers Bureau. Your notion is a good one and I'm sure that a number of the people you mentioned in your letter will be able to take advantage of the additional exposure your group could offer.

(continued)

(*continued*)

I appreciate being included in your list of speakers, but I will not be able to participate. Most of my speaking engagements are associated with our university, and I really do not have time for any further commitments.

Most sincerely,
Dean E. Smith

After my letter blitz, and the generous help of Kevin and Rick, I had amassed a database of over a hundred athletes' home addresses and phone numbers. Just having all that information compiled was something special.

Along with the invitations, we had sent out a brief survey asking about the athletes' personal preferences. When the surveys came back, I learned some valuable information about the players: the products they dreamed of endorsing; which ones wouldn't mind being paid in products such as car parts or stereos; who had issues with alcohol; even the practice schedules of their teams.

I knew this information could be my lifeblood.

I added all the information into a database on a Mac Plus computer whose $2,600 cost drained most of the $4,000 of the remaining Pepsi settlement. Then I printed a brochure that promoted the athletes for speaking engagements.

I would sit home at night and watch every channel on TV, to see which athletes were doing what, and read every paper and magazine to see which advertisers were doing what.

I filled scrapbooks with clippings of articles and advertisements that pointed to overlapping interests between athletes and companies—potential sponsorships. My eyes and ears were always on high alert.

When an idea hit me, I'd call a company's PR or ad department, and pitch them a player and a marketing plan. I was making this all up from scratch, but I called as many companies as I could, working *What Else's* from all angles.

Dreaming Up Appearances

In the late 1980s, Darryl Strawberry was one of the biggest names in sports, and I had a good relationship with him, dating back to my nights at the Hard Rock. I proposed to a local Ford dealership that they make a special edition model called the Strawmobile. Darryl would do an appearance at the showroom, sign autographs, and take photos with customers. I'd help them promote the event and the new model. I promised it would drive a lot of foot traffic to the dealership, more than they'd ever seen in one day at that location. People could bid on the Strawmobile; one lucky person would win it. Ford loved the idea and it turned out to be a huge success.

I was working with a great business model—representing not only the players and their interests, but also the companies and theirs. Rather than competing against each other, each party had a vested interest in promoting the events, seeing them succeed, and in splitting the money evenly enough so that all involved would be interested in doing future projects.

Oftentimes I'd pitch an athlete to a corporation for a specific event, and immediately afterward, the company would start to plan a slate of future events with me. In other words, that company would become a new client of mine.

There's no better way to get business than to give business. Help people sell. Drive accounts to them. When Ford saw how many customers Darryl and I brought them, they wanted to organize other promotions with me. (And sometimes I could even borrow a car from that dealership-if I needed to shepherd around a celeb who was in town for a day.)

* * * * * * *

In the late 1980s and early 1990s, there was a retail boom, during which stores like Walmart, Target, Caldor, Sports Authority, and Macy's opened a wealth of new locations. A host of new sporting goods stores also popped up.

These retail stores were eager to try new things and invest more and more resources to increase foot traffic. And they had both their own money and vendor money to invest in promoting events.

My old high school running mate Cliff Savage and I have stayed friends ever since graduating from Dewey. In the 1990s, when I was starting Steiner, Cliff became VP at Franklin Sporting Goods and was an invaluable liaison to the retail world. Utilizing his connections at Franklin, Cliff tipped me off to new mall openings and store expansions; then I would approach the managers with promotional ideas and proposals for player appearances. Cliff also introduced me to key people at stores like the Sports Authority and Herman's; with his help, I was able to get my business in on the ground floor of those stores before they became industry giants. Cliff was a tremendous influence on me; he taught me so many of the ins and outs of retail, and told me who to call at each company, to tap into that chain's marketing budget.

You never know where your friends are going to wind up. You can never imagine how they one day might be able to help you. (Yet another reason never to make enemies!)

THE UNDERSELLING IN SELLING

Though Cliff is a great salesman, his style is very different from mine. I'd try to sell a meat Popsicle to a vegan; Cliff goes with more of a "soft sell." In that way, we've learned from each other.

My favorite sales lesson from Cliff is that "It's not what you sell the customer; it's what the customer has left." In other words, don't oversell. If you convince someone to buy more than he needs, there's a good chance his inventory will be overstocked the next time you call on him. He won't buy from you on that call, and he might even look for a new sales rep—one who is more attuned to his needs.

Better to sell the client just enough, or even a little less than that. Give him a chance to get that "It sold out!" feeling.

Not overselling is an underrated part of selling.

I worked as many grand openings as I could, all over the country. And I conducted themed campaigns with the chain stores. A popular player would show up at several different stores in a region, and at each location, people would come to meet him while they bought their sneakers and their tennis rackets. It was the new big way of driving customer traffic.

Store events were really exciting to me. They were like puzzles; to solve them, I had to get creative. If a Nathan's opened up somewhere, rather than just having a player appear behind the counter, I'd have a Yankee do a fielding clinic in the parking lot. People would go wild.

One of my favorite promotions from the early days was an event we organized a few times with a pasta company, Ronzoni. I matched Ronzoni—which back then was one of the sponsors of the New York City Marathon—with renowned New York City restaurant Tavern on the Green. The night before the race, we'd have a huge party there. I'd bring in three or four name athletes, and the restaurant would serve a pasta feast. A lot of high-profile runners showed up to those dinners; it became a big event. World-class runners and celebs, carbo-loading side by side. Naturally, I took some of the runners on as clients.

MEDICINE MEN

One time I saw Mickey Mantle do a small advertisement for an arthritis cream. Watching Mickey talk about the benefits of the medicine, I realized that athletes had unique credibility when promoting products in the realm of physical health.

I surveyed every athlete I could get ahold of, to see which health issues concerned them or their family members. Then I went to pharmaceutical companies to see if they wanted to use a player to help promote awareness of a disease, or to get word out to doctors about a new product.

This led to several spokesman deals for athletes, including Johnny Unitas endorsing a prostate drug, and Earl (the Pearl) Monroe recommending a high blood pressure medicine.

Another promotion from the highlight reel was one we came up with for Pfizer, at a pharmaceutical trade show in New Orleans. The company's main goal at these events was to get doctors to learn about their new drugs. We had Hall of Fame running back Walter Payton attend one as part of the Pfizer team. He sat in front of their booth, surrounded by sports lockers. Above him hung a sign that read: DON'T RUSH BY. ANSWER FIVE QUESTIONS ABOUT THIS NEW DRUG, AND GET YOUR PICTURE TAKEN WITH WALTER PAYTON. Countless doctors stopped in their tracks, just to meet Walter. And since we made them answer some questions before getting their photo taken with "Sweetness," they were helpless but to listen to the reps' talking points. Pfizer quickly became the most popular booth at the show.

In another *What Else* twist, instead of just mailing out the photos, we had the area reps deliver them directly to the doctors' offices. That way they could further pitch the drug in person, and deliver samples.

Nobody else was really doing this kind of thing. Everyone wanted to cast Mean Joe Greene in the Coke commercial, but nobody wanted to be the guy arranging for him to go to a shoe salesmen convention in Scottsdale.

No matter what the product or promotion or cause, there was always an athlete that matched perfectly and helped take the thing to another level. For instance, a group of disabled Vietnam vets needed someone to speak about overcoming physical limitations. So I introduced them to Phil McConkey, a diminutive wide receiver on the New York Giants who seemed to have made it to the NFL purely on guts and heart.

It wasn't always the companies or organizations that had the need. Sometimes the athletes themselves had a need. For instance, we did some great work with Bob Mann, a golf pro who made instructional tapes. Professional athletes who played golf as a hobby were always looking to bring down their handicap. I pitched Bob on having them in his instructional videos. We got everyone from NBA Hall of Famer Oscar Robertson to tennis great Arthur Ashe. Each of them got professional golf instruction free of charge—or even received a small fee to participate. The athlete lowered his handicap; Bob had a dynamic new instructional tape to sell. The series did tremendously well.

I even heard from a lot of agents. As long as I wasn't going to interfere with the player contracts, or invest the athletes' money, I was an asset to them. They entrusted me to market their clients in ways they weren't equipped to do.

One of the most rewarding—and fun—campaigns I did in those days was with two icons from my childhood: the chocolate drink Yoo-hoo, and baseball legend Yogi Berra.

In the 1950s and 1960s, Yogi was Yoo-hoo's biggest pitchman, endorsing the drink via appearances in addition to countless advertisements. He even got his legendary batterymate Whitey Ford to join him in a few ads. The campaign was so successful that Yoo-hoo gave Yogi stock in the company—long before major sponsorship deals between athletes and corporations became commonplace.

But by the mid-seventies, after Yoo-hoo's ownership had changed a few times, Yogi and the drink were like oil and water. Stories about the breakup made it sound irrevocable.

In 1993, I was working on a promotion with Yoo-hoo that allowed customers to redeem proofs of purchase from the bottles to get a set of specially made Yoo-hoo Baseball Legends trading cards. I knew Yogi would be the perfect pitchman for it. But the current owners thought it would never happen. And they had good reason to have doubts.

> But I always need to hear the word "no," live and from the horse's mouth. And even then, I need to hear it several times. Up until that point, there's always a chance. And if you want to be a successful entrepreneur, that's the only way to operate.

Mickey Mantle graciously introduced me to Yogi, and I personally appealed to him and his wife Carmen to consider the Yoo-hoo opportunity. I knew I had to be patient; just as relationships take time to build, so do they require time to be repaired. I made sure to listen to all of Yogi's concerns, all of his qualms about moving forward. To quote the great Billy Joel, it was a matter of trust. Carmen was instrumental; with her help, I was able to convince Yogi to give Yoo-hoo one more chance. I promised him everything would go smoothly, and thanks to some hard work, it did. It ended up being one of Yoo-hoo's most successful promotions ever. They were happy, Yogi was happy, and I felt reassured that I had gotten into the right business.

Like I said, I blindly tried to get in front of as many athletes and companies as I could. I worked the phone day and night.

I called the company. I had the meeting. I called the player. I wrote up the contract. I picked up the athlete and delivered him to the spot. I sent the bill to the company. Then I moved on to the next promotion. At the end of the month, Mara came in and attempted to balance the books.

In the first few years that I ran my own shop, concentrating on fight nights and other "party" events, we had been lucky to organize five or six corporate athlete appearances per month (in addition to any ad campaigns we could get involved with). But starting in the early 1990s, our business model began to shift. We were managing between 100 to 200 events per month. No promotion was too small. We were doing around 2,000 appearances a year!

By this time, I had a young man named Andrew Levy working for me. Only two years out of college, Andrew was like a Mini-Me; he had stayed in touch with every person he had ever met, would work the phone all day, and could get "inside" information on anyone, long before the internet. Andrew was an excellent point man for countless athlete appearances, a true pillar of the Steiner Sports foundation.

MY JERRY MAGUIRE MOMENT

In those early, hungry days, during the football season, I regularly drove to Giants Stadium in New Jersey. Then I'd just hang around the parking lot, waiting for the team to finish practice.

As the players exited the building and walked to their cars, I approached them, pitching them my business. Ideally, I wanted to sign them as clients, but I was happy just to get a phone number; I was always looking to expand my roster of relationships.

I did my Giants Stadium parking lot routine for several years.

This approach really paid off for me in 1991, when the Giants won their second Super Bowl. By that time, I counted a large chunk of the team among my clients, including Ottis Anderson, the starting running back and a highly respected league veteran. I had competed with many other marketing agents to sign Ottis, and I held 100 percent of his marketing rights exclusively.

The Giants upset the Bills in the Super Bowl, and in running 102 yards on 21 carries, Ottis won the most valuable player (MVP) award. He was a seasoned pro, who just won the Super Bowl MVP, for a New York City team—you couldn't ask for a better guy to market, at a better time, in a better place.

I ran with it. I set Ottis up with countless appearances and signings, and I got him some good promotional gigs, including Nathan's and Amex. I showed him the money.

I might have incorporated the company in 1987, but this was the true beginning of Steiner Sports—the catalyst that said we were for real.

* * * * * * * *

People tend to get confused when they think about achievements. You have to be as excited about the tiny steps that add up to success as you are about the broader idea of reaching an ultimate goal. I had to be excited about my parking lot routine. If you can't find inspiration in little steps like that, it's going to be difficult to take the big steps you have your eye on.

Two years later, the Bills reached the Super Bowl for the third straight time, facing the Dallas Cowboys at the Rose Bowl in Pasadena. (Sadly, the Bills were well on their way to a record four straight losses in the big game.)

(continued)

(continued)

American Express was one of my clients at the time. They were hosting an MVC (Most Valuable Customer) Super Bowl Party for their upper echelon cardholders at the Playboy Mansion; they had us organize it. We arranged for a host of former Super Bowl MVPs to attend, including Marcus Allen, Roger Staubach, and Ottis Anderson. I desperately wanted there to be an even 10 MVPs there, but we could only wrangle up 9.

Then, the day of the big party, while I was waiting outside a hotel for someone else, I bumped into none other than Steelers great—and Super Bowl IV MVP—Franco Harris. I asked Franco if he would help us out, and he immediately agreed to attend the Amex party, no questions asked. True, it was an invitation to the Playboy Mansion, but over the years I've learned that it wouldn't have mattered if it was to the local library; Franco Harris is simply one of the nicest guys I've ever met.

When I picked him up that night to head to the mansion, Roger was already in the front seat next to me. Franco got in the car and started chatting amicably, but Roger wouldn't say a word to him the whole way there. It was stunning.

After we arrived and got out of the car, Roger pulled me aside.

"Don't put me in a car with a Steeler again," he said. "Those guys took two rings from me, and I will never like any of them."

Who says pro athletes don't take their jobs to heart?

OUR FIRST MAJOR DEAL

Despite all the hard work in the first several years, Steiner Associates didn't make any significant money until late in 1993.

I had five employees by that time, but I was still basically keeping the business afloat from project to project, trying to support myself one week or month at a time.

Then 7Up hired us for a promotion.

The soda maker wanted its vendors to buy more soda. Simple enough. We designed a contest for them. If a vendor met a certain threshold in its monthly order, it would win an autographed jersey or trading card of a star basketball player. We billed the campaign 7 FOOTERS FOR 7UP.

If you ran a deli or restaurant that sold 7Up, and if you ordinarily bought 25 cases a month, now you had incentive to buy 50—because that would win you an autographed, officially licensed Kareem Abdul-Jabbar jersey to hang in your store (or home), or a Larry Bird- or Scottie Pippen-autographed basketball poster to hang in your store (or home).

Until my team and I crunched the numbers, we weren't 100 percent certain of the cost of carrying out the contest: the estimated price per autograph, per photo, per jersey, and per frame—multiplied by the number of vendors and potential orders. When we finished costing it all out, we discovered that the total cost of goods was likely to surpass 1 million dollars. That was the first time we had dealt with a number that big. This was huge.

I gave the blueprint to the guy who did all our buying—an associate on whom I relied to orchestrate these kinds of campaigns.

"Brandon," he said, "I think that if the vendors buy a million dollars of products, we will make around $250,000 profit."

That was a lot of money. But in a way, it wasn't.

We were going to do a million-dollar project, and control every aspect of it, but we were only going to clear $250,000? It didn't add up to me!

I figured that if we could clear $250,000 on a promotion, it automatically meant that the campaign was big enough to squeeze even more business out of it. I took over the lead in negotiating the goods and services.

I went to a framing manufacturer—in lieu of the local framer we usually used for our work. I knew I'd get a better bulk price there. Then I asked some of my other customers if they'd be interested in memorabilia from these basketball players. Then I called each athlete personally and proposed that instead of signing, say, 100 items, that they autograph 200. Even though they'd have to take a little less money per item, they'd net a significantly larger sum on the back end—for not much more work. I also worked with the jersey manufacturers to get a better price there. We didn't know exactly what the final order would be, but I was confident that between the contest and the ancillary item sales, it would be large enough to scale the entire project up a few notches.

The project turned out to be a monstrous hit for 7Up, and Steiner Sports made around a $400,000 profit.

We had been so happy with the first $250,000, that we almost left the second $150,000 on the table. If you're working on a sizeable deal, you have to assume you have something even larger on your hands.

Sometimes success is less about finding new business than it is about taking what you have and putting it to better use. A lot of people would have been ecstatic with that original profit estimate. But to me that was a giant red flag, making me ask, "What am I missing here?"

You have to dig deeper. Look at every part of the project, and see if you can make more money on the margins.

Since I adopt this approach as much as possible in my life, a lot of my friends and employees think that no matter how well things are going, I'm never happy.

The truth is, I'm a tremendously happy guy. I'm living a great life.

I'm just never *satisfied*.

YOU NEVER KNOW

In 1994, Bill Liederman convinced me to change the name of the company from Steiner Associates to Steiner Sports. I had chosen the original name to give the business the imprimatur of an all-purpose marketing company. But as Bill pointed out, sports was our specialty and besides—the new name had a much better ring to it.

I didn't exactly start out with some grand plan to enter the sports marketing business. I started out in a completely different industry—food service. Even when I began working with athletes, I was booking them as bartenders and glorified party guests. The key—the unifying thread—is that at every step of the way, I was committed to doing the best job possible, and to meeting as many people as possible. The people I met and did business with saw how hard I worked, and in turn, opened up doors for me. But it was a real day-to-day grind, filled with ups and downs.

"You were a scraper," Mara tells me. "You'd get some work over here, do a little work over there. You were confident enough in yourself to go off to do wacky things and make them work. That's where you set yourself apart. Most people don't have that confidence; they have to stay in one place."

(Did I marry the right woman or what?)

It's a cliché, but in life you really have to keep your nose to the grindstone. It was around five years from the time I first incorporated Steiner Associates to the time I had my first real piece of business on my hands. If I had let myself become distracted, if I had given up at all during that time—if I had "looked up" from what I was doing—I might have missed any number of key opportunities.

PLAY THE GAME, NOT THE SCORE

When I coached my son Crosby's little league teams (which I'll get into more deeply later), I observed a vast array of motivational tactics on the part of the other coaches. For instance, sometimes when a team was winning but its players were losing focus, the coach would implore them to imagine they were getting pummeled.

"Play like we're 10 runs down!" he'd shout.

Now, I've watched a lot of baseball, and I can safely say that normally, when a team is *actually* down 10-0, its players don't look too motivated.

And to most people, a game with that kind of score is a boring show to watch. But I believe that it's actually the best reality show you can find. When a team has virtually no chance of winning, the game becomes a great indicator of who its great players are. I like to see who is still playing hard. Who's still launching himself out of the batter's box, scrapping his way to first? Who's still diving for balls? Who's still getting dirty?

Those are the committed players. The passionate players. The ones who realize that consistency over time equals credibility. The ones who know that ultimately to be successful, you have to give your all *all the time*, no matter whether you're winning or losing. That's the difference between being a real player and being a human thermometer. I've learned this from the most successful athletes I know. Hank Aaron. Mark Messier. Derek Jeter.

"Play the game," they say. "Not the score."

Derek Jeter is a perfect example of this mind-set. The Yankee captain plays hard during every inning, every pitch, day in and day out, over the course of the entire season. He doesn't let his fundamentals lapse; you can never tell what the score is from Derek's body language during a given game. Even in the last game of the season, watching Derek you wouldn't know if the Yankees were headed to the playoffs or if they were in last place in the American League East.

Entrepreneurs, employees—everyone—should perform the same way.

When you walk into your office, can you tell whether it's nine in the morning or six at night? Is it the beginning of a promising quarter—or is it the end of a bad month? Are employees' stock options riding a promising wave, or slogging through a trough? In reality, none of these factors should matter. A valuable employee will look like a valuable employee no matter the situation and circumstances. Consistency over time equals credibility.

My mother and mentor, Evelyn. Her favorite saying really was "You gotta have balls."

Cooking at Camp Sussex, one of my favorite places on earth, which I attended from 1975 to 1981.

It took me five years to get to this side of the kitchen, where I'd make the soups, stocks, and sauces. Cooking for hundreds was an invaluable experience.

A Sporting Club promotional from the early days of my celebrity bartender nights in January 1986.

Ron Darling was a very popular guy in New York. Little did I know that this was only the beginning of my working with athletes.

One of my first big Fight Nights, held at the 4D Club in Manhattan.

After I saw this idea through, from advertising to execution, I knew that I could be a successful promoter.

The first brochure that Steiner Associates did, in 1989.

David Cone was one of our first clients. The names listed are the athletes who first said yes to the invitation to join Steiner's Speaker's Bureau.

Rick Barry, Kareem Abdul-Jabbar, and me at a New York City party in 1990.

This was a party for Pat Riley's new book. As a basketball junkie, hanging with these two Hall of Famers was something special.

(L–R) Brooklyn Dodgers Ralph Branca, Joe Pignatano, and Clyde King; comedian Freddy Roman; Dodgers Cal Abrams and Clem Labine; me and Steiner employee Andrew Levy at Trump Palace in Atlantic City, 1991.

Trump Palace was looking to do a promotional event that would appeal to an older crowd. The promotions manager and I came up with the idea of doing a 1950s night with 1950s music, 1950s décor, and iconic 1950s Brooklyn Dodgers players. It ended up being a real hit and was one of my first "A-ha" moments in this business.

Here I am with Arthur Ashe at Le Coq Sportif Tennis Clinic in New York City, 1992.

I recorded a golf instruction video with Bob Mann and some other athletes, including Arthur. During the breaks in filming, instead of hanging out and hitting golf balls, Arthur sat down in a chair, writing something. I asked him what it was; he said he was writing a letter to numerous CEOs, like the head of Coca-Cola, explaining to them the different opportunities they had to do work within the African American community. I was impressed by his tenacity; that here on a beautiful day, Arthur was focused on doing work for other people.

Joe Namath never came to the office without going out of his way to say hello to everyone. He once told me that the two hardest things in life are walking into a room and everyone wanting your autograph—and walking into a room and no one wanting your autograph. Next to Mickey Mantle, Joe always had the nicest autograph in the business.

Here I am with Phil Rizzuto and Derek Jeter at the Turn 2 Foundation Dinner in 1998. This is a special photo to me because both of these great Yankee shortstops were in no small way responsible for helping make Steiner Sports what it is today. The Turn 2 Foundation is one of my favorite charities because it shows how committed the Jeter family is to helping kids.

My wife, Mara, and me at the American Cancer Society dinner in Westchester, 2000.

A thank-you note from one of my Little Leaguers. It doesn't get any better in life than receiving a note like this.

Dear Brandon,

Thank you so much. Thank you for taking me to the Yankee game. I had a great time at it. I can't believe that I got the foul ball, it was my first one. I had a lot of fun at the Mets game as well.

I had a lot of fun playing baseball this year. At the beginning of the year I wasn't sure that I even wanted to play baseball. At the end of the year though I'm glad that I did. You made the baseball experience so much fun. Thank you so much. I will always remember you as the most fun baseball coach.

THANKS.

One of my favorite years of coaching Little League. This was the first season I really had my bearings as the coach.

With Michael Jordan at Michael's Fantasy Camp in Las Vegas, 2001.

This was right after my squad beat Michael's in a four-on-four half-court game. It just goes to show that with preparation and focus, anything can happen.

I also spent time with Mike Krzyzewski at Michael Jordan's Fantasy Camp. This was right before I coached basketball in New Rochelle. I sat down with Coach K in the middle of lunch and I thought he'd scoot after 10 minutes; but he stayed and talked with us for two hours. He had such humility; if you didn't already know, you never would have guessed what a giant he is in basketball. When I told him about my dreams of coaching, he even invited me to watch a Duke practice.

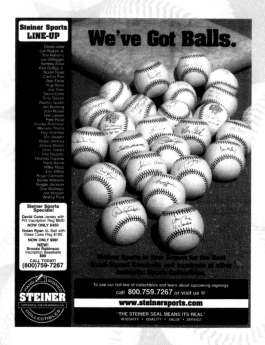

This billboard was one of our first promotional campaigns, in the early 2000s.

It wasn't tough coming up with that slogan; we had a lot of baseballs to sell!

Mariano Rivera and me at Yankee Stadium, 2002.

Mariano is one of those guys who, no matter how many times we've hung out, it always seems like the first time. We always have a very meaningful conversation. He's had a profound impact on my spirit, my faith, and the way I get my work done.

Here I am with Gary Carter, and my son, Crosby, in Scarsdale, in 2002.

Sometimes you forget how intense some people have to be to have gotten to the level they've reached. I saw it that day in Gary. He generously took time to give my son a catching lesson, but he couldn't turn off that intensity, and it ended up being a little too much for Crosby, who was too young to appreciate Gary's drive. That was my mistake; when you give a gift, you have to make sure the other person has the capacity to receive it.

With Cal Ripken at the National Sports Collectors Convention in Chicago, 2002.

Working with Cal was eye-opening. My company had arranged for a host of big athletes to sign autographs at this convention, and Cal noticed how hard I was working there to make sure it went smoothly. He said, "You're a lot like me; you're a thinker. You think everything over and over because you want to get it right, and I'm the same way." I had never thought of myself that way—as a thinker—so that gave me tremendous confidence.

With Charles Barkley at the Friends of Bill Russell Basketball Camp in Las Vegas, 2007.

I knew Charles would be friendly and personable, but his intelligence about the nuances of the game was what was really surprising. People get distracted by how entertaining he is—and he's very entertaining—and they don't realize how intelligent he is. It makes sense; to be as successful an NBA player as Charles was, he had to have a sharp head on his shoulders. Charles signed a few pieces for us, but I could never convince him to do a big line of collectibles. He just didn't believe in it, personally. He's one of the few guys I could never crack. Gotta respect that.

Joe Torre and me at Yankee Stadium in 2008.

Joe was another cornerstone of our company: he was there for us when we started our first serious lines of collectibles, in the 1990s. As the leader in that vaunted Yankee locker room, he could have used his influence to do any number of deals. He went our way, and I'll always be grateful for that.

With Derek Jeter at Yankee Stadium in 2009.

You can't be luckier than to have a relationship with somebody like Derek Jeter. His consistency, his selflessness—everything he does is for the right reasons. You can trust him 100 percent with anything.

Mariano Rivera and his son with me and Spike Lee at Madison Square Garden, 2009. (Photo courtesy of George Kalinsky.)

Brooklyn in the house: Spike and I overlapped for two years at John Dewey High School. Now we're sitting courtside at Knicks games. Don't tell us dreams don't come true if you work hard enough.

Here I am with Henrik Lundqvist, Amar'e Stoudemire, and Scott O'Neil, president, Madison Square Garden Sports, in 2010.

Madison Square Garden is the biggest venue in basketball and hockey, and, as a guy who grew up in New York, I knew we needed to have a memorabilia deal there. We struggled for a long time to work it out, but with the help of Scott O'Neil, we finally came out with our first items in 2010. This was a huge win for us.

Jay-Z and me in his dressing room before his concert at Yankee Stadium, 2010. That night, Jay-Z taught me the difference between being hot and being truly great. I could tell how much the crowd revered him; that's not going away any time soon.

(L to R) Reggie Jackson, Mariano Rivera, me, Dave Winfield, and John Sterling at a New Rochelle fund-raiser for Family Services of Westchester in 2011.

When you get guys who are great at what they do and committed to what they do, great things happen. Here, people were in the middle of bidding for a chance to win a lunch with Mariano, Dave, and Reggie. When Reggie took the microphone to drive up the bidding, things went to another level; you could see Mr. October.

Here I am With Mariano Rivera, Brett Gardner, and Joba Chamberlain at The Clubhouse Grill (Rivera's restaurant in New Rochelle) in 2011. (Photo courtesy of Anthony J. Causi.)

This was the grand opening party for The Clubhouse Grill, which also served as a fund-raiser for Family Services of Westchester, an organization close to my heart. Those guys came out for me to support it, and we raised over $300,000 that night.

With Magic Johnson and me at the Steiner office in New Rochelle in 2011.

Magic is one of the few athletes who can talk to management, salespeople, warehouse employees, and general fans, and express the same level of interest in all of them.

Mark Messier taught me the true definition of winning. He explained to me that winning isn't for most people; they don't want to go through the ups and downs, the trials and tribulations that are built into it.

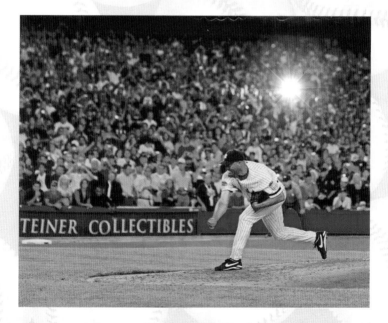

The last pitch ever thrown at old Yankee Stadium. (Photo courtesy of Jim McIsaac/Getty Images.)

The Yankees-Steiner sign was part of a board that rotated throughout the game, and we always had the ninth inning. Before the game, I told Mariano to step in front of our sign after he threw the final pitch, so all the photos of him would include that sign. "The scary thing is," he said, "you're serious right now."

In the Carrier Dome, at the Jim Boeheim Syracuse University Basketball Fantasy Camp in 2012, with a teammate and Orange legends (bottom left-right, clockwise) John Wallace; Derek Coleman; Steven Thompson; the pride of Brooklyn, Dwayne "Pearl" Washington; and Billy Owens. Our team had four of the greatest Orangemen of all time as our coaches; no wonder it was our second camp championship in a row!

Here I am interviewing Victor Cruz and Eli Manning after the Giants' 2012 Super Bowl victory. This was my second time interviewing Eli Manning for a (New York) "Times Talk." Every time I speak to him, I'm struck by Eli's focus and determination—and he's one of the kindest, most generous athletes we've ever represented. Victor is an amazing story himself: undrafted out of UMass, he's an NFL star who now owns New York City.

Giants Head Coach Tom Coughlin did a signing for us after the Giants' 2012 Super Bowl victory. Seeing Tom win two Super Bowls after four decades in coaching was gratifying for everyone who knows what a great coach he's always been. Coach was the offensive coordinator when I was a student at Syracuse, so having him sign for us also gave me the feeling I had come full circle. A really special day.

Interviewing Jeremy Lin in New York City, 2012. I was extremely nervous to interview Jeremy; not only was this during the height of "Linsanity," but he had graduated from Harvard! He was really funny and honest and put me at ease immediately.

Trust me; removing all the seats from Yankee Stadium was not easy. By the way, we still have some available for purchase. (A brother's gotta ask for a sale somewhere in his own book!)

Turning a bust into a boost: A section of the frieze looks epic in Chick Lee's yard, but very few people have the resources to accommodate it like that. The miniature model— made from the melted-down frieze—was a good way to deliver the magic to more fans.

EVERY DAY IS GAMEDAY

A few years ago, I was asked to give the keynote speech at the opening of the Xanadu Shopping and Retail Center at the Meadowlands, in New Jersey (now called American Dream Meadowlands). The ceremony was going to be held at a nearby college.

Being asked to give a big talk is always an honor. But when I saw the roster of speakers the organizers had lined up, I was even more excited than usual. Both the governor of New Jersey at the time, Jon Corzine, and the area's congressional representative, Steve Rothman, were slated to speak at the event as well—before me, no less. As I sat down next to those dignitaries, I really felt like I was in the Major Leagues. I was even more pumped as the event began, and I looked around the auditorium. The place was packed; there looked to be 400 people in attendance.

Midway through the event, however, my excitement turned to disappointment. After the governor, congressman, and the other speakers in front of me had taken their turns at the podium, the emcee announced a short break—during which a vast majority of the audience, including the VIPs, promptly left for good. Instead of speaking before the governor and other leaders in a packed house, I was going to be standing in front of a few dozen random people in a cavernous, empty hall. The wind went out of my sails.

But then I admonished myself. Didn't the small group of people who had stuck around deserve the same speech and effort from me that I was going to give the governor? Why would I compromise my performance on account of my disappointment? Wouldn't that only serve to make me feel worse about myself?

Who would gain from that tactic? No one.

I got up there and threw myself into the speech, full throttle. It went very well. I talked about finding the entrepreneurial spirit in yourself—how it's all about seeing the changes going on around you and finding the *What Elses* in them. After I finished and the event ended, a man came up to me.

"I loved what you had to say," he said, extending his hand. "I'm Mark Lamping."

(continued)

(continued)

I knew the name immediately. Mark Lamping was CEO of the New Meadowlands Stadium Company—and the former president of the St. Louis Cardinals. (Currently, he's president of the Jacksonville Jaguars.)

"I was looking forward to meeting you," he said. "We might need your help selling the old Giants Stadium, when the time comes. I'll be in touch."

In the following months, more than a few firms competed for that project; in the end, it went to Steiner Sports.

You never know when an opportunity is going to present itself—or who might be listening.

Too many salespeople misunderstand the unique importance of consistency. They have a big sales day, and to celebrate, they buy themselves a big lunch. Then, they leave work early because they feel they've earned it.

But where is the logic in this? Are you less worthy of good food when sales are down? Conversely, if you feel you have done well, why arrest that momentum by taking a break?

The days when you have a big sale—when you're riding a big wave—are the ideal days to go for a second big sale, and possibly a third. In my experience, the best time to make more money is when you're *already in the process* of making money. There must be a reason that that day has turned out successful. Harness it.

It's like a batter on a hitting streak, who's seeing the ball really well. He doesn't want to take a day off. He wants to ride that wave as long as he can.

When I was starting Steiner Sports and I had a good sales day, I never wanted to leave the office.

"Please don't let this day end," I used to think to myself. "Don't let 9 p.m. come too quickly. I need this day to be longer."

I didn't want time for a rewarding meal. I wasn't building my waistline. I was building a company.

In the hungry days at Steiner, our office was only two blocks from Madison Square Garden. My athlete connections afforded me a lot of Knicks and Rangers tickets, and during the basketball and hockey season, many nights after work I'd go to a game. And on most of those nights, I couldn't go home after the final buzzer. I had to pay dues to the work that got me those tickets in the first place. It may have been 11 p.m., or even midnight, but I'd go from the Garden right back to the office. Heck, back in those days, I would have swum the Atlantic Ocean to get to work. My company was exploding and I did whatever I could to ensure it continued on its upward trajectory.

Would you wake up every morning at 5 a.m.? Would you regularly return to the office after an event, half exhausted and stuffed with junk food, at 11 p.m. on a weeknight? You might think you're giving 99 percent of yourself to something, but being all in means giving 100 percent. Either you're all in, or you're not. The difference between 99 percent and 100 percent is 100 percent.

RELATIONSHIPS, NOT TRANSACTIONS

Playing the score and not the game is not only unwise business; it's not wise on an intrapersonal level, either.

Look at how we treat phone calls. Too often, if we call someone and leave a message, we don't even consider trying them again until they've called us back. It's phone tag.

Playing the game of life amounts partly to not worrying about everything being quid pro quo with everyone. If you need to speak to someone, give them a call. Even if you've already left a message.

As long as you're polite about it, what's the harm? The other person might even appreciate you taking the initiative, if they were having difficulty making time for a call themselves.

Similarly, once or twice a month, it's handy to go through the e-mails in your Sent box, to see if any important ones have gone unreturned. With the myriad ways of communicating that we have nowadays, it's easier than ever before for messages to slip through the cracks. So really, there's less reason than ever before to be offended by someone dropping the ball. E-mail them again!

Do as much as you can, for as many people as you can, as often as you can, without expecting anything in return. Don't worry about what you're getting back from someone you're giving something to. Don't worry about how many dollars that person is going to equal for you. It's counterintuitive, but there's definitely more joy in giving than receiving. There's a reason that's an expression, although you may not believe it until you've had the balls to commit to this mind-set.

Most people can't do it. They're too concerned with what they're getting back from the other person. But being generous with what you have without keeping score is the only way to live. It strengthens your spirit, it keeps you focused on the people who make your business what it is, and it helps breed success. And earning some good karma never hurt anyone, either. Having the right attitude will help you reach the right altitude.

I've always operated under this principle with the media, which is one reason I've gotten solid coverage over the years. Back in the 1990s, when I was starting Steiner, the sports marketing industry itself was in its infancy. Even the journalists who were covering it didn't really know too much about it. Whenever a reporter called me for a quote, or for guidance on a story, or to connect with the right person, I went out of my way to help them.

There was no e-mail, or Google, or websites. Phone numbers were hard to come by. I built a reputation as the guy who could get players on the phone with journalists—which made their lives a heck of a lot easier. I'd do whatever I could to help. And you can be sure that I wasn't getting much in return. But I was definitely accumulating credibility.

Inevitably, since I became such a trusted source, my name, and in turn, my company and brand, ended up in the media quite often. In the first 16 years of Steiner Sports, I didn't spend more than $150,000 on advertising, promotion, and PR combined.

That's unheard-of for the level of advertising, promotion, and PR we actually got.

Ultimately, it's important to remember that you might not always get paid in money for your actions or time; but what you do end up getting might in reality be something more valuable.

That's the irony; when you play the game, and not the score, you usually end up "scoring" more as a result.

TURNING MEMORIES INTO MONEY

EXPANDING OUR BUSINESS

ADAPTED FROM *THE BUSINESS PLAYBOOK*, PAGE 33:

Our collectibles business initially began as a tangent to the "celebrity appearances" side of the company. In advance of the appearances we arranged, we usually asked the athletes to sign some memorabilia; we would have David Cone sign a dozen baseballs, or ask Gordie Howe to put his John Hancock on a handful of pucks. We'd then send these pieces to corporate clients to get them to return our calls, or thank them for their business. Or I'd use them to help certain charities raise money. There were plenty of reasons to keep a stock of these items on hand.

Today such autographed pieces could cost us thousands of dollars, but they weren't as big a deal back then. And by 1993, we had built up a tremendous inventory of sports collectibles.

Meanwhile, as our appearance business grew, so too did requests for the "souvenirs" themselves. People called us and asked if we had, for instance, any extra Yogi Berra baseballs lying around. But it could have been anything. "You got this?" "You got that?" The calls kept coming and coming.

This was a big *What Else* in the making. It was as if—harking back to my paper route days—the milk had become more of a draw than the newspapers. Accordingly, we decided to start a memorabilia company, simply expanding on something that was already successful. It's not like we reinvented the wheel; we just put more spokes on it.

This meant expanding our business on multiple levels. We began producing and framing our own original photographs and ordering our own bats and balls for signings. Previously, we had outsourced these items, which cut into the profit margin of each collectible. Fittingly, the Sid Loberfeld monies came into play once again; I used the $10,000 in savings from the car insurance settlement (from my summer before college) to ramp up our capabilities so we could process all of our collectibles in-house.

Looking back at some of the twists and turns in my life, like the Pepsi bottle exploding and how that led to meeting Sid—with his sports collectibles, and the money that eventually helped me start my own collectibles company, it's hard not to see an invisible hand at work.

It's like the philosopher Joseph Campbell said: "If you follow your bliss, you put yourself on a kind of track that has been there all the while, waiting for you, and the life that you ought to be living is the one you are living."

But again, it all falls into place only *after* you've committed yourself to the path that's right for you—as opposed to the ones that fit others' false expectations, or even misplaced expectations you have for yourself. And "your bliss" doesn't necessary mean what's easiest for you, or what gives you instant gratification. It's whatever feeds your spirit and fills your soul. In fact, later in his life, Campbell speculated that a better way to put it might have been to say, "Follow your blisters." For me, it's always been about finding creative ways to bring services to people.

* * * * * * *

Once our collectibles department was up and running, we had to find other big name athletes to seed it with.

After I met Chicago Bears running back Walter Payton, aka Sweetness, through the Pfizer promotion, I booked him for other marketing deals. One weekend in the early 1990s, I was with Walter in Las Vegas, for Konica Cameras. The entire weekend I kept begging him to sign a bunch of footballs for our collectibles line, but he adamantly refused. He was the nicest guy in the world, but he wasn't a big autograph guy. And what can you do about that? Still, after the whole event was over, and we were on the way to the airport to fly back home, Walter agreed to do one signing.

A few weeks later, a few employees and I flew out to Chicago, where he still lived. Having not fully specified with Walter the exact definition of one signing, we wanted to make sure we could get as much as possible out of it. We packed a hotel room with 1,500 items: footballs, photos, cleats, Chicago Bears mugs, anything you could think of. He signed it all in less than an hour. All of it!

But that was nothing compared to 1999. That year, when Walter was dying much too soon from a rare liver disease, he agreed to sign 20,000 items for Steiner, to be sold only after he passed away. It was by far and away our most significant line of collectibles up to that point; it really put Steiner memorabilia on the map. I'll always be infinitely grateful to Walter for that.

Our second big "get" was Phil Rizzuto, affectionately known to Yankees fans as the Scooter. Born—where else—in Brooklyn in 1917, Phil grew up to be the starting shortstop on seven World Series–winning Yankees teams in the 1940s and early 1950s, earning the AL MVP in 1950. After he retired from baseball, he broadcasted Yankees games on radio and television for 40 years. Scooter was known for his distinctive, Brooklyn-infused voice, and his signature catchphrase, "Holy cow!" In 1993, he was announcing games for the local TV channel WPIX.

Although Phil was one of the first athletes I booked, he and I did not exactly get off on the right foot. I had hired him for a store appearance, but when he went to cash the $1,500 check I gave him as his fee, it bounced. I called the manager at my Citibank branch, a very nice guy named Mr. Gonzalez, to find out why. He and I previously had worked out a deal where he'd make sure my checks cleared, so long as I made up any difference to him quickly enough.

"How could you let my check bounce?" I asked him.

"I didn't!" Gonzalez said. "I made sure it went through."

"But Rizzuto said the check bounced," I said.

"Oh, yeah, that one bounced. You had one check made out to him, and one to Mickey Mantle. I could only cover one of them," Gonzalez said. "I had to go with the Mick."

Fortunately, that bounced check didn't negate the level of comfort and trust I had curried with Phil personally. He continued to work with me.

In 1994, after too many years of near misses, Phil was finally inducted into the Baseball Hall of Fame, thanks to Major League Baseball's (MLB's) Veterans Committee.

One night shortly after the announcement, I went to dinner at the house Phil and his wife Cora shared. Phil had never hired an agent before, but I wanted to be his first. I explained that his Hall of Fame (HOF) induction was sure to bring about a new surge in his popularity. "Everything is going to change now," I said. "You need a memorabilia and appearance agent to help you capitalize on it all. To bring you to the next level."

Wouldn't you know it—he agreed to sign with me, out of the dozens of agents who were courting him at that time. That was one of the biggest deals I ever made; Scooter's influence spanned the entire Yankees universe—something that would come in handy down the line.

At the same time, Phil never let me hear the end of that bounced check.

Another memorable signing we did in those nascent days, in the early 1990s, was with Lawrence Taylor. Similar to Walter Payton, LT was reticent to autograph merchandise and agreed to only one signing—at his house. We brought so many pieces for him to autograph that I had to rent a truck just to transport it all. I convinced Kevin Heller to join me in driving out to meet him. After we got to the house and brought in all the items, LT began signing everything. But, after a little while, we heard another car pull into the driveway.

"Shoot," LT said to Kevin and me. "That's my marketing agent."

Apparently he had another guy who was supposed to handle these types of things, and if he saw us, there would be trouble. LT had Kevin and me hide in the closet until he left.

Hiding in that dark closet with Kevin for the sake of some autographed footballs and helmets felt a little unsettling, but it also reinforced my feeling that this—sports memorabilia—could be a huge industry.

At some point LT let us know the coast was clear, and we finished the signing. The whole experience was exhilarating.

MY FAVORITE COLLECTIBLE

By this time, Mara and I had been married for eight years, and we had started a family. Our son Crosby was born in 1991, and in 1994, we welcomed his sister, Nicole.

One night when Crosby was little, as I was tucking him into bed and getting ready to read him a story, he asked me what my favorite piece of memorabilia was. I had never specifically articulated the answer to myself—let alone anyone else—and Crosby's question got me to think it through.

Hanging in my office at home, I have a framed photo of Mark Messier holding the Stanley Cup in his arms, wearing the most ecstatic smile you've ever seen. The picture was taken just after the Rangers' Game 7 Finals victory over the Vancouver Canucks in 1994.

Mark, a good friend of mine, inscribed on the photo: "We did it!" This is my own favorite collectible.

"I think it's because that photo highlights an important period in my life," I told Crosby. I went on to explain that the Rangers' win came at a very emotional time for me. My mom had just died, which was incredibly painful. But at the same time, I had two amazing little kids that I was getting to watch grow up with my loving wife. My business was doing well, and I expected it to really take off, thanks to the success of Mark and the other Rangers whom I had as clients. I had worked months to sign Mark; in fact, he was the first athlete I ever signed to a collectibles deal, specifically. I knew my labors were about to pay off big time.

Around the time that photo was taken, as I sat in the Garden watching the Rangers celebrate—seeing how happy they were, and how happy their fans were, myself included—a flood of emotions ran through me. At that moment, watching Mark hoist the Cup, I felt life itself very deeply. It was like a religious experience; I was truly inspired.

The next morning, on the train into Manhattan, literally everyone in my car was reading a New York paper; each one had that shining photo of Mark and the Cup on the cover. I had rarely, if ever, experienced an event that brought together New Yorkers in that way. I knew I was going to have Mark autograph a photo for me, and I wanted only three words on it: We did it. I knew that every Rangers fan, having suffered through a 54-year Stanley Cup drought, would have understood that sentiment completely.

After explaining all of this, I looked down, expecting to see my son's glowing face. Of course, he was asleep. I realized I had been talking for quite a while; I had lost myself in reliving that moment at the Garden.

Crosby's question changed how I viewed memorabilia. Instead of merely being a collectible, each piece held the potential to be a totem—a magical gateway into the past. The difference between my own Messier photo and another copy of the same photo was the inscription—Mark's words are what unlocked that magical potential. They were the unifying force that brought together the visual image and the emotions I felt at that moment.

I thought that every fan had to have their favorite sports moment, and that moment must be one of the top ten moments in their whole life. I knew that the right photo, the right collectible, could conjure up those feelings again.

The next day at the office, we began brainstorming other collectibles that begged for inscriptions. Joe Namath writing "I guarantee it." on a magazine cover featuring an image from Super Bowl III, or Franco Harris writing "The Catch" on a photo of the Immaculate Reception. We could have Louisville Slugger replicate the bat Bucky Dent used to smash the infamous home run over the Green Monster against the Red Sox in their one-game playoff in 1978, and Bucky could inscribe it with "The pennant-clinching homerun." We could reproduce the hockey stick Wayne Gretzky used in his rookie season, and have him personally write the year and his stats from that season on it. We could even have Bill Buckner inscribe a photo of his infamous moment in the '86 World Series with "Oops."

We were going to create product lines that revolved around not just players, but players and *moments*. A Reggie Jackson–autographed baseball was nice, but a Reggie-inscribed ball, referencing his three-homer World Series Game in 1977, contained an entirely new dimension.

We were the first to market with this kind of product, and Mark Messier and the '94 Rangers had been the perfect cornerstone upon which to build this new business. It was a fantastic *What Else* moment, and the first of two big tipping points for Steiner Sports.

During that time, I would come home from work talking a mile a minute about all the opportunities that popped up that day, all the people I had met, and all the new projects that were just getting started. Mara would roll her eyes.

"If only one-third of these things end up working out," she'd say, "wouldn't that be something."

Then Extel, a financial data-communications company where Mara worked was sold, and she got a year's salary as severance. So we decided she should join me at my office. "I'll come in for a month or two," she said.

That very first morning she came to work, Mara made the business radically more productive and professional. Right off the bat, she looked at the motley arrangement of computers we had and explained how we could network them and share resources more efficiently. Unimpressed by our phone-answering procedure, which consisted of an impromptu game of hot potato every time the phone rang, Mara also insisted we hire a receptionist.

Mara is almost single-handedly responsible for bringing Steiner into the information age.

She even convinced me to get a postage meter. I had always been paranoid that if I bought one for the office, everyone on staff would use it for their personal letters and our mailing costs would go through the roof. I needed Mara to knock some sense into me on things like that.

Perhaps most significantly, Mara executed a real financial plan for Steiner Sports, and she showed me how to get a line of credit from the bank. Previously, I had had a visceral aversion to borrowing money (a model that carried with it benefits like bouncing a check to my boyhood hero Phil Rizzuto).

From the time of our first major ascent in the industry through our purchase by Omnicom Media, Mara served as CFO. She kept everything in order, in a way I never could. A stickler for documentation, Mara watched every dime. We couldn't come back from a business trip with an expense report that was even two dollars off. She'd be all over you until you could explain the discrepancy.

"I bought a pretzel in the airport," I'd plead. "I just forgot to write it down!"

For Steiner Sports, Mara was just what the doctor ordered.

A year after she started working with me, she came into my office smiling.

"I think you have something here," she said. "This could really be big."

Signing some big-name athletes had been encouraging, but when Mara said that, I knew we were really on our way. Going on 15 years now, Mara has been the voice of reason at Steiner, the one to get me to see the light when I've gone into one of my trances. Her office is three doors down from mine.

So in addition to being the love of my life, the mother of my children, and my emotional and spiritual rock, Mara's long been the glue that holds Steiner Sports together. The company wouldn't be half of what it is today without her.

AS MEAT LOAF SINGS, TWO OUT OF THREE AIN'T BAD

Sometime in the late 1990s, as Steiner was beginning to really get off the ground, I was in Orlando with Jim Kelly, Hall of Fame Buffalo Bills quarterback. I had accompanied Jim down there for two appearances he was doing at a big sports memorabilia trade show. One night he took me out to a local bar, and at around 2 a.m., while Jim and I were chatting with some people, I felt a tap on the shoulder. Turning around, I recognized one of the top collectors from the show.

"Brandon," he said. "I know you are starting to really grow, and I like what you're doing. But remember. There are three pillars of business—price, quality, and service." He paused. "And you can only excel at two."

To this day, I try to run my company with service and quality as the main goals.

THE BIG BREAK:
YANKEES-STEINER

In 1999, Steiner Sports really started to roll. That year, we signed a multiyear deal with Derek Jeter. We also had an exclusive deal with Mariano Rivera by the time he won the 1999 World Series MVP, after the Yankees swept the Braves in four games. And in 1999, we signed Mia Hamm to the first ever collectibles deal for a female athlete.

By opening day of the 2000 Major League Baseball Season, Steiner Sports represented most of the players on the Yankees *and* the Mets. So when the two New York teams finally met each other in the World Series that October—a dream come true for every New York baseball fan—we were in position to offer a collectible to all fans of the game, no matter which team they were rooting for. It was like we were in the middle of a perfect storm, and we were the only ones selling umbrellas. The Subway Series was another tipping point for Steiner. It garnered us a priceless amount of attention, and we did our best to capitalize on it;

with the help of my old friend from Brooklyn, Steve Stein, we set up an online auction of Mets-Yankees memorabilia—the first such web-based auction Major League Baseball had ever seen. At the same time, we were bursting with new collectibles lines, and booking talent all over the country. 2000 was a dream year.

But a few months after the World Series ended, I received an ominous call from a VP of Major League Baseball, Howard Smith. Smith was in charge of licensing and was my contact at MLB. He informed me that Yankees officials were asking questions about Steiner Sports—and me in particular. They had made a lot of calls. They had reached out to Louisville Slugger, the Home Shopping Network, the Yankees Store, and other vendors and accounts we worked with. They had even spoken to a couple of players.

One core of our business comprised baseballs, bats, and other equipment we had autographed by big name players, including several Yankees. Apparently, the club wanted to know how we were attaining these products—and the parameters under which we were selling them to certain stores. Did we have the proper rights to do this? I don't know that the Yankees management thought I was bribing batboys to sneak equipment out of the clubhouse; but suffice it to say, they had questions about how I was sourcing the merchandise I was selling. They also knew many of their players were doing events with me, and spending time on other Steiner projects. They weren't thrilled with that either.

In reality, Steiner by that time was working directly with MLB licensees like Rawlings and Louisville Slugger. They manufactured gloves and bats specifically for our players to sign: high quality Steiner originals, truly worthy of the Yankees brand. And we sold these only through official MLB retailers. Everything we were doing was on the up-and-up, and totally legitimate.

Then, in the spring of 2002, I bumped into my old buddy Billy Rose, after a game at the stadium. In addition to the Sporting

Club and his other restaurant ventures, Billy happened to be a limited partner in the Yankees. I'd been his guest in the owner's suite at several games. But this time, we ran into each other in the parking lot.

"Hey, Billy," I said. "How's it going?"

Billy looked a little grim.

"I don't want anybody to see me talking to you," he said, looking around. "Your name is coming up around here a lot. You should be careful."

Whoa.

"Be careful about what?" I asked.

"Just in case you're doing something you shouldn't be doing," he said. "They're asking around about you."

Apparently, the powers that be were still a bit suspicious. I was on George Steinbrenner's radar, but not exactly in the way I had dreamed. It seemed like a good time to meet with the club, to remove the shroud of mystery once and for all.

Besides, I had long wanted to get my foot in the door there. This was as good an opportunity as any. The question was how to approach the club.

I had a good relationship with Derek Jeter's agent, Casey Close. So rather than reach out to the Yankees directly, I wanted to go through Casey. He had credibility with the club and *I* had credibility with him—after doing right by Derek ever since he put his trust in us by signing that multiyear deal.

If you want to get to somebody—or some organization— that's hard to reach, go through someone close to them. Work the back channel.

Casey delivered. A month later, I was scheduled to meet with him, Yankees General Manager Brian Cashman, President Randy Levine, and COO Lonn Trost.

As the meeting with the Yankees brass approached, I was nervous. Scared to death, actually. Were they angry with me? What was I going to say? *Are they going to take away my season tickets?*

But once we started talking, I realized there had been nothing for me to be afraid of. They were very nice and congenial, if not a little guarded.

The three officials simply wanted to know more about the Steiner Sports operation. They explained that my name kept popping up when they asked vendors how all these Yankees players' collectibles were coming up for sale online. The club wanted to make sure their fans weren't getting fake, or otherwise substandard, pieces from me. I had nothing to hide, but I understood their concern. How could they trust someone they didn't know? They were all about protecting the Yankees brand.

"I'm not just freewheeling in this business," I explained. "In fact, Steiner was purchased by Omnicom." (Omnicom, a leading holding company in the marketing and communications industries, that has over 500 companies under its umbrella, bought Steiner Sports in 2000.)

I figured that if the Yankees knew that Steiner was part of the Omnicom family, they'd know that I had to have been operating according to the highest standards. Indeed, the Omnicom name went a long way toward putting them at ease.

Seeing how protective these gentlemen were of the Yankees brand, I immediately saw an opportunity, a *What Else* for the Yankees.

"If you have any questions about what's going on with your merchandise out in the marketplace," I said, "I can be your eyes and ears. I know this stuff better than anybody. Whose products are legit, who you can trust—and who you have to be careful with."

They were receptive to the proposal.

Then the conversation went in directions I could not have anticipated. We drifted into a more detailed discussion of Steiner Sports' own capabilities.

This was where Casey really came through. Again.

"I represent Derek Jeter, and he's one of the biggest names in baseball," Casey said to Randy, Lonn, and Brian. "We could work with anyone in the collectibles business. We have a lot of choices. But we work with Brandon. I can't think of anyone better suited to representing the Yankees brand."

Casey explained that Steiner was not only doing a great job with Derek's collectibles and licensing; we were also giving him a great deal of assistance with his Turn 2 Foundation, which supports programs that help young people turn away from drugs and alcohol and develop healthy lifestyles. Helping Derek with Turn 2 was never part of our official contract with him but we worked on it because it was important to Derek.

Trust and relationships.

"The reality is, you can't beat Brandon Steiner," Casey went on to say. "And if you can't beat him, join him."

Sensing my cue, I jumped in.

I never lack for ideas, so I immediately began listing them enthusiastically—how the Yankees could partner with Steiner Sports to sell things like game-used jerseys and equipment. Autographed bats and balls. Appearances and signings. Official photographs.

"We could offer dozens of products we probably can't even imagine right now," I summed up.

"This sounds promising," Randy said. "Let's set up another meeting."

I was very excited.

IT'S NOT WHOM YOU KNOW, OR WHAT YOU KNOW, BUT WHAT YOU KNOW ABOUT WHOM

In addition to collecting memorabilia, I'm a huge collector of people. Of course, there are a lot of people who know a lot of people.

However, the effective people distinguish themselves by making the most out of those connections. It's not whom you know, or what

(continued)

We spent the next several months creating in-depth proposals for *official* Yankees-Steiner products. We had several more meetings. All in all, the talks went on for about two years.

The deal was complicated; it encompassed players, player products, the YES Network, MLB licensing, retailing, concessions. We spent countless hours talking collectibles with Randy Levine as well as Scott Krug, Yankees CFO, and Adam Raiken, Michael Tusiani, and Marty Greenspun, Executive Vice Presidents. Each detail had to be blessed by multiple departments in both the Yankees organization and Major League Baseball. Lonn and Randy, along with Omnicom CFO Randy Weisenburger, came through big time; those men worked hard to get all the pieces to fit together.

Randy Levine took the initiative in developing a Yankees-Steiner collectibles show on YES, which would be instrumental in promoting the new line. Brian Cashman even had me speak at a team meeting in the clubhouse, to explain the Yankees-Steiner partnership to the players. I got to speak to the Yankees in the clubhouse—can you imagine! I was also touched by the knowledge that George Steinbrenner himself had blessed the deal.

Throughout the process, what intrigued me most was how much time the Yankees put into understanding what *we* did.

They were unbelievably thorough. They asked countless questions about the collectibles process—from the sourcing of the merchandise, to the way it would all be shipped and stored. The Yankees wanted to fully protect against a counterfeit product with their logo entering the market, even 30 or 40 years down the road. They insisted on working very closely with the folks who run the MLB authentication program. A half century from now, there might be no civilization as we know it, and no professional sports, but if there is a Yankees souvenir baseball lying in the post-apocalyptic dirt, you can bet it will be authentic.

What other company would have its most senior executives spending so much time learning about a retail product line? It would be more lucrative to ease up on this level of diligence, to spend a little less money on processes like authentication. But the Yankees showed such genuine concern over all the ways that our projects might ultimately affect their fans.

There's a reason their fans are so dogged. The Yankees earn that fealty.

The Yankees-Steiner partnership was finalized in the fall of 2004 (right before the Yankees playoff collapse versus the Red Sox—more on that later). The deal was officially announced that December.

The press conference at the stadium felt like a second Bar Mitzvah—an entrance into a sacred, timeless society. I had become a part of something, a little sliver of the Yankees organization. My wife and kids were there; I was glad that they got to see the culmination of the work that had so long consumed me, and at times taken me from them.

Along with the Yankees officials, Derek Jeter, Mariano Rivera, and Joe Torre were in attendance. As usual, Joe was as warm as could be. We didn't grow up together, but I'm sure he was proud to see another boy from Brooklyn make good. Mo was dressed casually, and Derek busted his balls the whole time, for not dressing up.

At the end of the presser, Derek pulled me aside.

"I'm here for *you* today," he said. "I'm very happy for you." What a feeling that gave me.

The Yankees-Steiner deal was one of the biggest deals the industry has ever seen. I'm proud to say that; it changed the way players, teams, and leagues looked at collectibles.

I'll never forget the day I went with Sean Mahoney, our EVP of team partnerships, to pick up the first wave of Yankees game-used jerseys that we'd be selling. Never before had anyone made available to fans a full collection of authentic, game-used jerseys from which they could pick and purchase their favorites. We were about to change all that! Plus there were all the other authentic items from Yankee Stadium we were going to sell—everything from bats to the decades-old steamer trunks the jerseys came in. Back at the office, when we unpacked those trunks of Yankee treasure, I think everyone at Steiner felt pretty proud. We were a part of something special.

So many other teams now have collectibles programs, featuring lines of game-used products and artifacts from stadiums. Yankees-Steiner was ground zero; our deal sent the message that these kinds of product lines are here to stay!

With many clubs, a deal can fall flat on its face if the team hits a losing streak or has a couple of mediocre years. But the business model we forged is sound enough to keep going strong, whether the Yankees win, lose, or draw. That model is underpinned by the forward thinking of the Yankees organization.

In the last decade, they built not only a stadium, but also a TV network (YES). They routinely execute first-of-its-kind deals. They see well beyond the New York market, and well beyond the here and now.

The Yankees could have WHAT ELSE? inscribed in giant capital letters around the top of the Stadium.

THE LIGHT IN THE
OTHER ROOM

In the fall of 2004, we were on the cusp of *officially* launching Yankees-Steiner. We were entrenched in the Yankees. When the team was one out away from winning Game 4 of the American League Championship Series (ALCS) and sweeping the Red Sox, with Mariano on the mound in the ninth, I had been projecting some wild numbers in my head. I assumed they were going to move on and win the World Series; with all the buzz and euphoria of another New York championship, we were going to make a killing. Among other potential windfalls, it was the first year Alex Rodriguez was on the team; so many of our bets were going to pay off. Yankees-Steiner was going to leap right out of the gate, and we were never going to look back!

So when the Red Sox came back from 0-3 down to rip the ALCS away from the Yankees that October, I was crushed. I was really in a state. I know it was like that for every diehard Yankees fan, but I had the added joy of preparing to watch my newest and biggest deal—the apex of my career—disappear.

The manner in which the Yankees lost the pennant that year was a collapse of historical proportions. It was the only time a team had come back from a 0-3 deficit like that—ever—and the Yankees were the victims. While the Red Sox celebrated their ALCS Game 7 victory on the Yankees' own field, I wondered if we were going to make a single dollar. What Yankees fan would want to memorialize *this*? It was like the lights got turned off in my soul. Just like that. Bam.

Don't get me wrong—I wasn't counting on the Yankees winning the World Series every year to sustain Yankees-Steiner. But this was about as bad a start to a new business venture as I could imagine. I just didn't think people were going to be very interested in buying Yankees memorabilia at that point. I knew how painful the Sox series was for me, so I knew the kind of effect it was going to have on like-minded Yankees fans—the same people I had been counting on to support the new business.

I felt like the Yankees had taken a huge chance on me. We spent two full years negotiating Yankees-Steiner. I had been living and breathing it. It had been a dream come true. I never wanted to wake up. I wanted to show the Yankees the money—right away. Now I feared I'd be showing them the losses.

I went into a little coma for a week.

By the time the Red Sox were up 3-0 against the St. Louis Cardinals in the World Series, I had mostly come to. But I was still a bit depressed and sluggish. The whole office was. We were a sorry bunch of salespeople.

A staff usually reflects the demeanor of its manager.

Then, in anticipation of Game 4 and the baseball season coming to a merciful end, I had a realization that would have made my mother proud.

As bad as it was for Yankees fans just then, it was the best thing that had ever happened to Red Sox fans. Those people suffered from untold sorrows and angst, and with the Red Sox finally beating the Yankees—*and in the way they did so*—I could only imagine the kind of euphoria Sox fans were feeling.

When your world gets dark, it's very tough to step back and say, "Wait a minute, there could be a light on in another room." It might be the toughest *What Else* challenge in life. But if you can find that other light, it's probably going to help you climb out of your hole.

So I did the only thing I could think of doing. I got my ass up to Boston, and I started shaping up the Red Sox-Steiner partnership.

> No matter how bad things seem, there's always some good hidden in your situation. Try to view it from an opposite vantage point, and you'll find it.

The Steiner team stepped up. We went crazy. We had to sign as many Red Sox players as we could, to get as many Sox deals done as possible, before the team won the Series, when we'd be shut out of the market. We worked 24/7, midnight shifts. We went full throttle, and ended up cornering the whole market. It was a proud moment for all of us.

That fall turned out to be a huge success. That year is still the best sales year we've ever had . . . thanks to the loyal and hungry Red Sox fans. We sold over 3,000 collectibles, each signed by one or more members of the team.

We even sold the home plate from Game 7 of the ALCS, at Yankee Stadium. That plate felt a little like kryptonite to me—I wanted nothing to do with it. But that just proved how much someone else must have coveted it. We pulled it from the ground right after the game, and the whole Red Sox team signed it, with the inscription "The curse was reversed." It fetched $210,000 for us. Not bad for such a depressing artifact.

* * * * * * **

After the World Series had ended, it was important to me to sign *every member* of the 2004 Red Sox team. There would be no end to the kinds of items fans would want to buy to commemorate a victory for which they had waited for so long, and I felt we needed every player to ensure they'd all be available. It was so important to have the entire market covered.

While a vast majority of the players were relatively agreeable, pitcher Curt Schilling kept holding us up for more money. He was extremely difficult to interact with, but I still wanted him because I thought we needed *everyone*. Curt had been a Major League star for a long time. I thought about the famous bloody sock he pitched with during the Yankees series, and how much he seemed to have enmeshed himself in New England. I thought Curt would be loved forever and a day in the region. So we caved to his demands.

To this date, it's the most we've paid to an athlete for that type of deal.

Unfortunately, we were so swept up with covering all our bases that we didn't take the time to do the due diligence to truly see if the Schilling base was worth it.

As it turned out, it wasn't.

In the end, Curt didn't have the kind of lasting popularity we need for our business. Many of his items are still gathering dust on our warehouse shelves. Curt Schilling was the one touch of gray on the Red Sox silver lining.

The mistake would have been excusable had we not had to pay Curt so much up front. His outsized demands were a red flag—a reason to pause, step back, and do the right research. But we were rushing so much at that point, trying to get everything done so quickly, that we didn't—and we're still paying for it. Around the office, we have a slang term for a deal that appears to be more hassle than it's worth: a Schilling.

Sometimes your best deals are the ones you don't make. Occasionally, working hard on a deal ultimately leads to scrapping it. Better to do the work and let the thing go than voluntarily tie an anchor around your own neck.

When the Yankees collapsed, I thought we were toast. Then we rebounded and reached great heights with the team that sunk the Yankees. But even that turnaround carried a major problem, in the form of Curt Schilling, that I wouldn't have expected.

It just goes to show you—you always have to be on your game, always ready to see the silver lining, always be ready to bust out Plan B.

Nothing ever comes out as planned.

Nothing.

TURNING DIRT INTO DOLLARS

I 'll never forget the last day at the old Yankee Stadium for many reasons, but one image may stand out more than any other.

In the moments after that game against the Orioles ended in a Yankees win, several of the Yankees and Orioles players bent down, scooped up a little infield dirt with their hands, and put it in their pockets. Some of them even came out of the dugout with little buckets.

Picture it. Mariano Rivera and Derek Jeter and Yogi Berra—on their knees—scooping up dirt like little kids.

Some people know me only as The Guy with the Dirt.

It's not the most prestigious title, but the truth is, I'm proud of our dirt. Steiner dirt is quality. It's authentic dirt!

It started in the 1990s, when I was first building Steiner. We were a small company. We didn't have a research and development (R & D) department. We had me, wandering around supermarkets, malls, stadiums, card shows, and Walmarts, to see what was going on in marketing and retail. That's something I do to this day.

Anyone who sells products has to regularly visit malls, and go to trade shows, street fares, bazaars, flea markets, bodegas, and garage sales. You never know where your next great inspiration might come from.

While attending the National Sports Collector Convention one year, I met a guy who was selling dirt from the first Marlins game at Joe Robbie Stadium. Little bottles of dirt, labeled appropriately, $9.99 each. I've always loved stuff like that. When the Colorado Avalanche won the Stanley Cup, I bought hockey pucks that had melted ice from the rink inside. Oddball things hit a nerve with me. I never know what I'm going to do with them, but I like to accumulate them. I'm a pack rat. And the more obsolete and obscure the items, the better. I placed the little bottles of dirt on my desk.

I stared at them. I didn't really understand the appeal at first.

But after some time, I found myself thinking: "It would be nice to own some Yankee Stadium dirt."

I remember the first time I had the privilege of walking on the field at Yankee Stadium. It was such an honor—one that most Yankees fans never get to experience.

But if I could get actual dirt from the field, I could give a small piece of that experience to anyone who wanted it. A piece of the field that, small though it was, was 100 percent authentic.

When I first asked the Yankees for field dirt in 2005, they didn't quite understand the request. But they were agreeable.

We played around with the various ways we could turn the dirt into a keepsake. First, we sold little capsules of dirt, glued to framed photos of players. Then the products became more intricate. We matched up specific dirt to specific players. We took shortstop dirt and paired it with Derek Jeter items.

Of course, we had everything authenticated. Independent MLB authenticators oversaw the dirt being extracted from the field, as well as its insertion into the capsules. That might be the most important part of the whole process.

As the economy began slipping into a recession in the latter half of the 2000's, our dirt items, which were more modestly priced than our other collectibles, began to really take off. So we dreamed up new products to expand the line even further. Dirt from specific games. Dirt with specific players. We sold dirt from all over Yankee Stadium. Dirt from the infield, outfield, and from around home plate and the pitcher's mound. Dirt from two inches below the surface, to as deep as two feet down. We sold over three tons of authentic Yankee Stadium Dirt.

We sold dirt from certain stadiums.

Fenway Dirt, Wrigley Dirt, Notre Dame Dirt.

Perfect Game Dirt. Playoff Dirt. World Series Dirt.

We created a collage with a map of the United States, and a little disk of dirt from every stadium in its proper geographic place.

We sold a hollowed-out Louisville Slugger with dirt from Derek Jeter's 3,000th hit game at the Stadium. Autographed by Derek, of course.

Half of our dirt is stored in barrels in our warehouse, for future use. The other half is divided into half-ounce portions that are allocated in discs, plaques, keychains, paperweights, collages, clocks, coasters (in case you want to serve a *dirty* martini), and countless other souvenirs; 360,000 collectibles in all. We look at all of our items to see if they can be paired with dirt.

Steiner Sports has sold $20 million of baseball stadium dirt over the past few years—$10 million from Yankee Stadium alone.

Not long after the dirt took off, we thought, "Why stop at dirt?" So we took some of the Yankee Stadium field grass, replanted it at a sod farm, then freeze-dried it and warehoused it. Fans can buy a little slice of the last field at the old Stadium—and it lasts a lifetime. Can you imagine having a little patch of Yankee Stadium center field on your desk at work?

Just a few months after we started selling our field grass products, I learned that officials at the Rose Bowl, the BCS Championship, and other college bowl games were going to sell patches of those fields. It's always gratifying to come up with a product from scratch, develop and market it, and then see it emulated by others.

I'm always ready to go right up to the edge of the cliff, when everybody's rolling their eyes and telling me not to jump. The more people don't see something, or don't agree with it, the more interesting it becomes to me—and, the more I enjoy the process of developing that market and activating it.

Steiner has sold 1 million dollars' worth of grass.

A JEWISH KID MEETS
TOUCHDOWN JESUS

While partnering with the Yankees fulfilled my lifelong dream, I wasn't dead yet. I still had a company to run, and I knew there were more opportunities to bring fans closer to their heroes. I had to find the next thing that would fuel our business.

After I find a new opportunity, I like to ask myself, "What did I miss here?" It's kind of like asking, "What Else can I do for myself?"

In this case I was thinking, "Is there another brand comparable to the Yankees?"

"What is it that makes the Yankees so special?" I analyzed. "They have a rich history. They have prestige. People who don't even follow baseball know who they are."

The only other team I could think of that had these qualities was Notre Dame football.

Many people might think the next logical step, after signing the Yankees, would be to sign another New York team, or another baseball team. Or at least, another well-known pro team.

But I wasn't looking at it that way. I'm in the business of selling history; that's what makes the stuff I'm known for. I can't only consider brands on account of their current popularity or geographic influence. First and foremost the brand has to have history. It has to bring out emotion in people.

That describes Notre Dame's relationship with its fans exactly. Like the Yankees, the college football program has a long, rich history, renown, and a stadium held sacred by many.

The only problem in adding Notre Dame collectibles to the business was that Notre Dame said no to everything. They're Notre Dame and they're doing just fine. Sure, they're aggressive with their brand; they want to be on top. But they can afford to be very, very picky.

Nonetheless, I figured Notre Dame might have seen that the Yankees had partnered with Steiner Sports, and having just inked that deal, it was a good time to go after them. We were hot.

But there was another problem: I've never been a Notre Dame fan. I watch them, and I respect them, but I bleed Syracuse orange, not Notre Dame green. I'd be lying if I pitched to Notre Dame and claimed to be passionate about the school (as opposed to the brand). And they'd see right through me. How many times a year does Notre Dame get proposals from people coldly looking to capitalize on that brand? This couldn't be a business deal that added up only on paper. It had to add up in the hearts and minds of the organization as well. I had to find a way to earn their trust.

One of my sales guys at the time was Pete Kelly. He was a Notre Dame lunatic—passionate about the team and the school. I knew he was going to be important here.

"Better to have a guy named Kelly call Notre Dame," I told Pete, "than a guy named Steiner."

Pete worked some magic, and eventually he connected with Boo Corrigan, now the athletic director at West Point, but at the time the associate athletic director in charge of corporate relations and marketing at Notre Dame. Boo worked closely with Scott Correira, who runs Notre Dame Sports Properties. Winning these guys over was going to be essential to completing this deal.

On their initial call, Boo told Pete, "We don't do things like this at Notre Dame."

Now, this isn't the first time I've gotten that response. It's gotten to the point where, if people *don't* say something like that, I get worried my idea is all wrong. And as a Steiner salesman, Pete felt the same way.

Despite their response, we sent Notre Dame information on our business. I had a few follow-up calls and they liked what we had to say. They were aware of what we had done with the Yankees after all, which gave us credibility.

There comes a point in business deals, though, where you need to meet in person. And, if you're waiting for that invitation, especially when dealing with a powerhouse like Notre Dame, that fields dozens of proposals every day—you're never going to get it. You have to step up.

We had to fly out there. Wherever "there" was. I couldn't have located Notre Dame on a map. I just knew it was somewhere in the Midwest. Somewhere between New York and California, there was Notre Dame Stadium. *Touchdown Jesus.*

So one January morning in 2005, Pete and I woke up at the crack of dawn and made a two-flight trek to Indiana: Westchester to Chicago to South Bend.

Scott picked us up at the airport in South Bend and drove us to the campus. We went to lunch at Legends, a University-operated restaurant just a few yards away from Notre Dame Stadium. It was a nice lunch, but I was antsy. I knew we had to get in front of Boo, the right hand to Athletic Director Kevin White, who was ultimately going to have to bless the deal. I didn't schlep out to Notre Dame, in the middle of nowhere, for a pesto turkey wrap.

Scott gave us a tour of the campus. It was beautiful. It took me back to the first time I visited Syracuse—that feeling of needing to be there, to be a part of it.

Then we got to the stadium.

For a Jewish kid from the streets of Brooklyn who's been obsessed with sports his whole life, I felt like I had died and gone to heaven.

We walked through the locker room, touched the legendary PLAY LIKE A CHAMPION sign, and stepped out onto the field. The stadium was empty, but that only made it more impressive; it was cavernous, like a cathedral.

I asked Scott about possibly putting up signage for Steiner Sports at the stadium if we were to get a deal done. Scott chuckled. He pointed to a spot in the distance, and we saw one small sign, for NBC Sports. That was it, in the whole stadium. No advertisements, no jumbotron—nothing. Nothing standing in the way of all of that history. This was not the type of arena I was used to.

The silence was deafening.

I looked up. Towering above the rim of the upper sections, I saw the Basilica of the Sacred Heart, the golden dome of the main administration building, and the Hesburgh Library with that famous mural of *Touchdown Jesus*.

I was completely in awe. But I was also completely nervous. I was about to have one of the biggest meetings of my life. If I closed this deal, it would be another milestone for Steiner. Notre Dame. You can't top that brand.

But what did they need me for?

I looked up at that 134-foot-high Jesus statue, with his arms outstretched. "Man," I thought, "I'm not in Flatbush anymore."

Meanwhile, Scott kept telling us that Boo was running late.

Before I knew it, it was 4 p.m. and we hadn't met with him. I was beginning to think it just wasn't going to happen. They certainly didn't seem overly excited to meet with us. It began to feel like we were being brushed off.

I soon started to worry that we might miss our flight out of South Bend. I couldn't think of anything worse than not meeting with Boo—or having a bad meeting with Boo—and then being stuck at Notre Dame for another day, trapped in the shadow of Touchdown Jesus.

Finally, Scott got a call from Boo's office; he was ready for us.

* * * * * * **

As excited as I was, I reminded myself to keep my expectations modest. I told myself that our goal was simply to start a relationship with Notre Dame, not to make a sale but to become friends.

Usually in a pitch meeting, I begin aggressively, describing the myriad things Steiner Sports can do, and how we can't wait to start doing them all immediately. We break out the PowerPoint presentation, with the charts and graphs, showing how we're going to increase the client's revenue and expand their customer base. Sometimes we try to show the client that we know their business even better than they do.

But in the end, you have to be cognizant of where you fit into the order of things. A brand like Notre Dame had more to teach us than the other way around, and we'd be better off letting the meeting go where *it* wanted to go.

Notre Dame football is a battleship, not a schooner; it can't turn on a dime. If we tried to ram through all our ideas in the initial pitch, Boo and his team might well think, "Who needs all that?"

Instead, my only objectives were to keep the dialog going, to keep them open minded about what we could do for them and, at the very best, to get Boo to come see us in New York.

> Sometimes it's wise to slow down and not link ambition and speed. In business, you have to know your place in the order of things.

Notre Dame had to be a slow play. We had to come across modest. We had to show them we could be a lineman, not a quarterback. When the meeting finally started, I saw that Boo and Scott had assembled the perfect group. The head of licensing, the lead equipment manager, and another key associate were there. They'd all be key people in a deal like this.

To begin, Pete and I emphasized a few of the strengths of Steiner Sports. We didn't propose that these strengths would necessarily come into play for Notre Dame, at least not right away. We told them we wanted to walk before we ran—to start off slow, with a couple of sample lines. We showed them framed photos of great Notre Dame moments, faux-signed by program icons like Jerome Bettis and Joe Montana; a collage of photos of legendary coaches including Knute Rockne and Lou Holtz; and game-used jerseys. We even floated the idea of selling replicas of the PLAY LIKE A CHAMPION sign.

Then, we let them talk, making sure to listen to what they wanted and needed. Maybe there were opportunities for us to work together that we hadn't thought of yet.

As we ended our discussion, Boo and his team explained that Notre Dame has an incredibly strong alumni base and that they were intrigued by the prospect of using it as a built-in sales network. They also really liked our licensing capabilities.

That was a start but there was more to discuss, and we had made it very clear from the beginning that we wanted to move slow. We just needed them to come back for round two.

"We'd like you come to New York to see our operation," we told them. "You need to see how we do things up close. How creative we are. How authentic our products are. If you can't come right away, we'll do it next year. We'll do it in three years."

No deal should ever make or break you, and we made it clear this wouldn't.

"You seem like good guys," Boo said, wrapping things up. "I promise I'm going to come to New York to see you."

As we were leaving, Pete asked to use the restroom. Boo told him he'd walk him there; Pete suggested that he point out the right direction to him instead.

"We don't point at Notre Dame," Boo said.

On the flight from Chicago back to New York, Pete and I were seated across the aisle from each other.

I was still buzzing from the meeting a couple of hours before. I leaned over to Pete. "How do you think we did?" I said.

"Why not us?" Pete said.

Exactly. Sure enough, three weeks later, Boo called us. He was going to be in New York, and he wanted to visit.

When he came to our office, now in New Rochelle, and saw what we were doing for the Yankees, Boo was blown away. It's one thing to impress someone with a story or a pitch. It's another thing to actually show them what you're made of. Seeing us up close went a long way towards Notre Dame's ability to understand the business and really trust us—to see us as a company that could do justice to its history and brand. Now, they could see us as a worthy partner as opposed to an opportunistic profit seeker.

I was glad that, back in Indiana, I had made it my priority to establish a relationship with the school, rather than to close any kind of deal. This was the strategy that worked.

"Now that I see all this," Boo said at the end of the Steiner tour, "I see a bunch of stuff we could sell right away."

Still, there was no reason to rush.

"Understand that with anything we do, we're going to move really, really slowly," I said. "One step at a time. Let's start off on solid footing, and take it from there. We'll get to everything, but let's do it right."

Before he left our office, Boo hugged me. That's when I knew we had a deal.

I imagined Touchdown Jesus smiling down, arms raised.

"It's good!"

* * * * * * * *

Over the course of the entire Notre Dame pitch—from the first Pete Kelly phone call, to the reserved meeting on campus, to the visit at our office in New York—we maintained that we wanted to build a relationship with them, not make a sale. We really listened to what Notre Dame wanted, and not to our own voices and assumptions.

We're competitive at Steiner. We can be ferocious salespeople. But we need and have the ability to be patient as well.

Soon enough, guess what happened.

Notre Dame started asking us "*What else?*"

In fact, one of the proudest moments I've had at Steiner was when I received an e-mail from Boo Corrigan a little while after we finalized our deal. In it, Boo wrote:

The Steiner Effect has reached our bookstore, where they plan to incorporate a specific area for the Notre Dame-Steiner Collection in the expansion of the bookstore planned for April of 2008. Again, a win-win for all.

Remember, early on this relationship was met with great skepticism on campus and now, we are getting calls from top offices looking for something special (i.e., Steiner Sports items) to send [to their friends and associates]. Great stuff! [e-mail edited for context]

It was so satisfying to learn that as a result of our hard work and patience, our vision had resonated not only with the Notre Dame athletic department, but with the rest of the school as well. That proved to me that more than *selling* Notre Dame, Steiner Sports had *done right* by Notre Dame. The latter is the only way to build a lasting relationship with a business partner.

I have met many individuals that have a tough time finding that equilibrium of ambition and patience at work. They mean well, but once you let them out of the cage, they start running a mile a minute, and soon they're out of control.

That kind of approach will never work with a brand like Notre Dame.

They don't even point there.

THE FINAL DAYS OF YANKEE STADIUM

I t was September 20, 2008, and the Yankees were hosting the Orioles one final time. It was going to be a big day for Steiner Sports.

Before the first pitch, dozens of players from both teams came up to me to request certain pieces: signs, seats, lockers; assorted odds and ends. Some players even texted me their requests *during* the game!

I was sitting in a field level box along the third base line, with my son Crosby and a few friends. The air was warm, the sky was clear; it was the perfect fall afternoon. Except for the guy sitting next to me, in the adjacent box.

He looked to be middle-aged, and he was wearing tan pants and a blue shirt; he was dressed like he was part of the grounds crew. The *entire* game, he kept hassling me.

"Are you gonna sell the scoreboard?" he said. "Are you gonna sell the pitcher's mound?" He wouldn't stop.

"What else are you gonna sell?" he kept saying.

I politely ignored him.

After Mariano Rivera secured the final out of the 5-3 Yankees victory, Mr. Tan Pants leapt out of his seat and *onto the field.* He made it out there before the police even had a chance to set up a barricade.

Tan Pants ran straight to third base, squatted down, and pulled it out of the ground like a weight lifter hoisting a barbell. Then he ran right back to our section.

As he was stepping over the railing, I extended my hand as if to help him. Then I plucked the base from under his arm, instead. Before the guy had a chance to react, the entire section erupted in a cheer.

"Caught stealing!" someone yelled.

Everyone went crazy.

With all eyes on him, Tan Pants didn't go back to his seat. He fled the section, running up the steps and through the closest exit, before security could get to him. At least he was empty-handed.

I went back to my own seat and sat down. I looked around the stadium, trying to pinpoint those old seats we used to sit in when I was a kid, the ones with the obstructed views.

I took a deep breath; I was very relieved. I couldn't have stood there while that guy stole something from me.

That's right, me.

When that final game ended, I basically owned Yankee Stadium and almost everything in it.

I'll explain.

YANKEES PLAYERS' STADIUM DEMOLITION REQUESTS

Mike Mussina

- His 6 season tix seats (Section 211, row E 1-6)
- His locker plus facade
- One of the large Yankees logos on the columns in the clubhouse
- Flagpole with the bat and flag
- Pitcher's rubber from his last start
- Table from the lounge
- Photo of Ruth/Gehrig from the lounge
- Photos from hallway of Ruth hitting and DiMaggio hitting
- Yankees banner from weight room

Derek Jeter

- His locker
- DiMaggio sign in dugout
- locker chair

Brian Bruney

- Two stadium seats #2, 3
- Facade above his locker

Jose Molina

- Two stadium seats

Joba Chamberlain

- Two stadium seats #6, 2
- Locker chair
- Facade above his locker

Carl Pavano

- One stadium seat

(continued)

(continued)

Cody Ransom

- Base from last home stand

Ivan Rodriguez

- Two stadium seats

Joe Girardi

- Two stadium seats # 11,12

Johnny Damon

- Two foul poles
- 10 stadium seats
- Locker plus facade

Alex Rodriguez

- Locker plus facade

Robinson Cano

- Two stadium seats

Tony Pena

- Five stadium seats

Mariano Rivera

- Bullpen bench (outside)
- Bullpen pitcher's rubber
- Locker chair
- Pitcher's rubber from his last game

Hideki Matsui

- Two stadium seats
- Home plate from last home stand
- Locker chair and name plate

(continued)

(continued)

Jorge Posada

- Locker plus facade and chair
- Two stadium seats
- Home plate from last home stand

Andy Pettitte

- Two stadium seats
- Banner from weight room
- Pitching rubber from his last start

Jason Giambi

- Two stadium seats
- Locker plus facade

Phil Hughes

- Two stadium seats

Gene Monahan (head athletic trainer)

- Eight stadium seats

By the time we were crossing the t's and dotting the i's on Yankees-Steiner in 2004, it was common knowledge that the organization was also finalizing plans to build a new stadium. Which meant that the old stadium was going to be torn down.

I wanted to buy the priceless remains, from the foul poles to the lockers to the bullpen bench. I wanted every seat and every sign—and of course, every patch of dirt and grass.

Each of these items, big and small, made up the building in which Ruth, Gehrig, and the rest of the 1927 Yankees played their home games. It was where DiMaggio once roamed center field. Where, in 1956, Don Larsen pitched the only perfect game in World Series history, methodically mowing down the Brooklyn Dodgers, one by one. Where Mantle and Maris slugged it out for the regular season home run record in 1961. Where Reggie blasted three homers on three consecutive pitches to clinch the Series against the Los Angeles Dodgers in 1977. Where Aaron Boone became Aaron (Bleeping) Boone.

Yankee Stadium held the aura of a cathedral. Going to a game there was like going to a religious service for me.

I wanted to collect all of its sacred relics and deliver them to as many devotees as possible. I thought we could sell it all.

I wanted Yankees fans to own pieces of the wall on the left-field line that Derek Jeter famously dove over like a kamikaze, headfirst into a bank of photographers and cameras, just to snag a blooper off the bat of Red Sox Trot Nixon. I wanted them to be able to purchase the clubhouse carpet George Steinbrenner and Roger Clemens once stood on, spraying each other with champagne. The desk on which Joe Torre wrote dozens of World Series game lineup cards. Just thinking about his stuff gave me goose bumps!

Your old seat, the one you finally bought season tickets for, from which you used to look out at the perfectly manicured field on all those Bronx nights.

In preserving these totems from the wrecking ball, we'd also be preserving a very substantial part of people's lives. We had to treat it like your grandmother's home—respectfully, delicately. Every little piece had a meaning and a story.

This was going to be the most difficult project Steiner Sports would ever undertake. For one thing, the politics were incredibly tricky: While the City of New York owned the stadium itself, the legal extent of the scope of that ownership was somewhat ambiguous. Who owned the actual seats in the stadium? What about the locker rooms? While we had been selling Yankee Stadium dirt for years, the City technically owned the land the stadium was built on.

We had to divide all of this up, for the purposes of determining a price—and to determine which things we could take away in our trucks, and which had to be left to the city.

I'll spare you the details, mostly because I wish I could have been spared the details. The negotiations between the City of New York, Yankees-Steiner, and MLB went on for months, and they weren't always "friendly." We haggled over everything. The City drove a hard bargain. The fact that the stadium was so close to so many subway lines made the situation additionally complicated—and expensive. You have to be very careful when demolishing a stadium whose foundation is entangled with multiple subway tunnels.

In the end, if we wanted the stadium, we were going to have to pay the City of New York $11.5 million. On top of that, we were going to have to pay $5 million in various construction and demolition fees, for a grand total of $16.5 million for the project. This level of investment was unprecedented for us.

Initially, not everyone loved the idea. The costs were higher than any deal we had worked with previously; to many people at Steiner, it didn't seem possible that we would ever earn our investment back, let alone turn a profit.

But I knew we had to have it. For years, I had poured my heart and soul into my partnership with the Yankees, and into building my company. Now we had the chance to buy the deconstructed Sistine Chapel, and to reincarnate it with a unique product line. It couldn't possibly get any better than that.

It could work. It had to work.

I mean, what was I going to do—wait for the next Yankee Stadium demolition?

After about two years of tough, complex negotiations with the City of New York and MLB, our $11.5 million deal to buy the demolished stadium was finally announced.

PRESS RELEASE FROM THE MAYOR'S OFFICE "MAYOR BLOOMBERG AND NEW YORK YANKEES ANNOUNCE AGREEMENT ON SALE OF YANKEE STADIUM MEMORABILIA"

Sale Brings $11.5 Million in Guaranteed Revenue to the City and Once-in-a-lifetime Opportunity for Fans

Mayor Michael R. Bloomberg and the New York Yankees today announced an agreement on the sale of seats and other City-owned memorabilia from the original Yankee Stadium. The City will receive a guaranteed payment of $11.5 million from the Yankees, and the team will sell the City-owned memorabilia together with Yankees-owned memorabilia through Yankees-Steiner Collectibles, the exclusive provider of game-used memorabilia from the original and current Yankee Stadium. Memorabilia owned by the New York City Department of Parks & Recreation includes Yankee Stadium seats, bleachers and fixtures such as the foul poles, player lockers, and the iconic "frieze." The City's proceeds from the sale will go to the City's general fund. The Yankees will be responsible for all contracting and costs related to the removal, sale and marketing of the inventory. Information on acquiring memorabilia from the original Yankee Stadium will be released by Yankees-Steiner Collectibles.

"The original Yankee Stadium has served as the place for some of baseball's most enduring memories," said Mayor Bloomberg. "Countless New Yorkers and people around the world have a lasting connection to the Stadium thanks to the legends who played in pinstripes, the plays that brought championships home, and even the popes that celebrated Mass there. I'm glad the City's agreement with the Yankees will generate much-needed revenue for the City, and offer fans a chance to own some of the famed Yankee Stadium history."

"We are delighted to have reached an agreement with the City of New York," said New York Yankees Chief Operating Officer Lonn A. Trost. "The original Yankee Stadium was—and still is—an important part of our country's sports heritage, and we are thrilled to be able to offer our fans the opportunity to acquire a keepsake from our former home."

Even if we didn't break even financially, I knew owning the old Yankee Stadium would do wonders for Steiner; it would legitimize the brand even further. I also knew it would get us a gold mine of free publicity—and it did. The amount of coverage we got when we held the press conference announcing the deal was greater than anything we had ever experienced.

It was picked up in dozens of papers and magazines nationwide, including the *New York Times,* the *Daily News, USA Today, New York Magazine, New York Post, Newsday, San Antonio Express-News, Seattle Times, Sports Business Daily,* and the *Boston Herald.* And it was covered extensively on TV—earning spots on CNBC, Bloomberg TV, and ESPN's *Baseball Tonight,* as well as radio mentions throughout the country, in markets including Houston, Atlanta, San Antonio, and Cleveland.

The phones in the office started ringing off the hook—and they didn't stop for days. There was a frenzy of interest. There's no telling how many new customers that wave of publicity brought us.

> Some of the best deals don't add up on paper; they're about capturing people's hearts and minds more than their money.

One of the first special requests I got was for the men's room urinals. It would prove to be the first of many.

Everything is priceless to someone.

I wanted to sell the urinals, of course. We got some surprisingly good offers for them, but the Yankees didn't want the urinals, let's say, contaminating the rest of the products. I had to pick my battles, and saving and selling the decades-old toilets wasn't one of them.

Although Yankee Urinals does have a ring to it.

* * * * * * *

I was there the first day of the demolition, when the trucks began pulling up to the site, to take the royal treasure away. There were no markings on the sides, but I was proud to know that they were Steiner trucks.

YANKEE STADIUM REINCARNATION

The most enjoyable part of the demolition project was gathering the Steiner sales team almost every day, for months, and just sitting around and brainstorming the Yankee Stadium product line. We were experienced dirt sellers; as far as we were concerned, everything was on the table. No idea was dismissed outright for being too far-fetched.

KEY STATS:

Items included in the Original Offering, 2009:

Joe Torre's office chair—$500

Eddie Layton's Stadium organ—$25,000

Yankee locker room chairs—$250

Home plate—$2,000

Home plate from last home game of final season—$200,000+

Giant "NY" logo sod behind home plate—$50,000

Monument park brick—$149

Bleacher seat—$40

Stadium seat pair—$1,500

Commemorative single seat—$750

(continued)

(continued)

Additional Items: American League team flags from top of stadium; ticket booths; entrance turnstiles; dugout bench; the batting practice cage; seats from George Steinbrenner's box; section signs; All-Star Game banner on the frieze; loudspeakers; Phil Rizzuto Banner hanging outside by the Stadium Club entrance; mini flagpoles on top of frieze; 26 World Champs sign; upper roof message boards; Jeter dive wall (three sections); seats turned into barstools

Most Popular Items:

1. Seats
2. Dirt/Grass
3. Goldrick bricks from original stadium construction
4. Signage
5. Seatbacks (painted, autographed, etc.)
6. Foul Pole Pieces
7. The Black Pieces
8. Lockers

Players Who Bought Their Own Lockers: Alex Rodriguez, Jason Giambi, Hideki Matsui, Derek Jeter, Reggie Jackson

There were items we always knew we were going to sell, like seats, bases, and lockers—a number of them signed by current and former Yankees. But there were also less orthodox pieces that we realized could be collectibles only after scrutinizing the stadium. That's when we have the most fun at Steiner—when we dream up new collectibles. New ways to bring fans closer to their memories.

The following are some of the more interesting Yankee Stadium product stories.

THE FRIEZE

On my desk, I have a replica of the front side of the original Yankee Stadium, as it looked in 1923. It's the color of sand, slightly opaque and grainy, like the old time era it represents. Even though it's small—the size of half a toaster—it's fairly heavy. It's one of my favorite Steiner products. That little model and I have a history together.

It all started with the facade.

To me, old Yankee Stadium was all about the frieze, or the facade as it came to be known. The signature feature of the House That Ruth Built wasn't flashy, like the Green Monster in Fenway Park, or the ivy and brick outfield wall of Wrigley Field. But it was no less distinguished—a 15-foot high white frieze, sitting above the bleacher section like a crown. I don't remember the first time I saw it, but I know I've looked for it ever since. I loved stealing a glimpse of it from my car every time I passed the stadium on the Major Deegan Expressway. Its pillars echoed the Yankee pinstripes. Simple yet regal.

In 1923, when Yankee Stadium first opened, the facade was copper and ran along the entire upper deck of the grandstand. Osborn Engineering, the Cleveland-based firm that designed the park, installed the frieze to give it an air of magnificence. They didn't copy its distinctive look from another building; it was completely original. If you ask me, they were right on the money.

When the stadium was renovated in 1976, the original facade was taken down to make room for 10 extra rows of seats at the top of the upper deck. The copper was sold as scrap. The concrete replica frieze that was erected and placed beyond the outfield wasn't quite as majestic as the original. But it towered over its share of Yankee dynasties in the late 1970s and late 1990s. It was still the most distinctive part of the stadium.

There was no way I was going to let the facade be sold as scrap this time. Plus, I thought it would be an instant hit.

What wealthy Yankees fan wouldn't want a section of the facade in their backyard?

I was dead wrong.

For one thing, it ended up costing half a million dollars to remove the frieze, section by section, making sure each concrete frame was preserved. It was an insane amount of work. Seeing that facade come down was like watching the "Crane Olympics." Then, after that ordeal, we were left with 10 slices of the frieze, each one 10 feet high at the ends, and 12 feet long—*and weighing 20,000 pounds!*

We had to set the price at $50,000 apiece just to break even.

Of course, considering the cost of transporting one of those sections, any married man who wanted a piece of the frieze couldn't possibly get it home without getting divorced. I don't know that we could have *paid* most people $50,000 to take one off our hands.

Only one person ended up buying a section of the frieze— Chick Lee. Chick is the CEO of a top media buying company, Icon, and a huge Yankees collector. He has a beautiful house in Augusta, Georgia, where the Masters is played. He wanted to put the frieze in his backyard.

You don't want to know what it cost to get that hunk of concrete down to Georgia. Chick needed a flatbed and a crane just to move the thing an inch.

I tried to talk Spike Lee into buying a section of the frieze for his country home, and there was a time when I thought he was close, but he ultimately decided against it. I *suppose* he did the right thing.

Thousands of years from now, the world as we know it might be unrecognizably transformed, but a piece of the old Yankee Stadium frieze will still be standing where Chick Lee's backyard once was. And people will stare at it like Stonehenge.

And Steiner Sports might still be losing money on it.

Happily, a few months after the demolition, we came up with an idea that would help recoup some of the facade losses.

We found a company to crush the frieze and melt it down. The mixture is poured into molds, and the end product is a scale model of the front of the original Stadium. Like the one on my desk. Ninety-nine bucks a pop.

These models might not cancel out the cost of the frieze on paper. But we took a big loss and turned it into a cool product, and in the process, found yet another way to deliver a little piece of magic from the old Stadium to Yankees fans.

Actually, as of this writing, it looks we might make some money on the frieze, after all. We currently estimate that we'll sell 20,000 units. That would be a million dollars in sales—on a mistake.

Still—if I could do it over again, I wouldn't go near the thing.

THE ORIGINAL BRICKS

Born in Haverstraw, New York, in 1850, Philip Goldrick came from a line of brick manufacturers. In the course of continuing the family business, he revolutionized the industry in the Hudson Valley. At the turn of the century, thirty million bricks a year passed through his factories and brickyards in Kingston. A towering entrepreneur and community leader, Goldrick built an entire hamlet for his 250 employees in Ulster, New York. Known as Goldrick's Landing, it was composed of homes and stores of the most modern design, and even boasted a beautiful Catholic Church. Phil Goldrick obviously knew how to ask *What Else?*

Goldrick's son Thomas rose to become production manager of the firm, and his other son Merton ran the sales and finance side. In 1922, producing red building brick exclusively, Philip Goldrick & Sons was the largest individual manufacturer in the Hudson Valley, and operated its own fleet of barges to ship bricks to New York City.

One of Philip Goldrick & Sons' biggest projects was the original Yankee Stadium. The firm supplied all of the bricks used in the original park.

I wanted those bricks badly.

Except we couldn't find any of them.

We had to submit to the contractors several lists detailing the pieces we wanted to save, and where they were located. We combed the stadium, up and down. We singled out seatbacks, concession signs, and lightbulbs. We took entrance turnstiles and even found speakers for Bob Sheppard, Yankee Stadium's venerable announcer, to sign. We put a hold on everything but the kitchen sink. I felt that if something important wasn't saved from the garbage heap, it would be my fault. I had a responsibility to Yankee fans like myself. But every brick we saw turned out to be from the stadium renovation in 1976.

A few days before the demolition was set to begin, my search carried me into the batting cage in the basement.

The batting cage was housed in the Columbus Room of the stadium. That was an informal name, as in, "If you don't get your swings in, they're gonna send you back down to Columbus (home of the Yankees triple-A team)." The batting cage wasn't exactly state-of-the-art; in fact, it was a pretty decrepit-looking facility. Anybody who saw it knew that the Yankees were overdue for a new stadium.

I was in the Columbus room, looking around, when all of a sudden I noticed the ceiling was composed of faded red bricks. It was them, I thought—they had to be the originals. I grabbed one of the contractors and asked him if he could take a brick out. Sure enough, the other side was stamped GOLDRICK.

Countless parts of a stadium are naturally replaced in the course of nine decades. And the 1976 renovation made sure that most of the original Yankee Stadium was lost to the dustbin. In my eyes, the Goldrick bricks were the closest thing to finding the butt of one of the Babe's old cigars, smoldering in an ashtray. I know it sounds corny to speak lovingly about a brick, to say a brick is sexy—but this is about as nice a brick as you're ever going to find. It's a sacred cathedral brick.

We found around 5,000 Goldrick bricks in total.

THE "I WANT TO THANK THE GOOD LORD FOR MAKING ME A YANKEE" SIGN

Early on, even before the first pencil had been removed from old Yankee Stadium, Derek Jeter made it clear to everyone that he wanted the iconic sign that hung above the entrance to the Yankees' dugout. Painted blue with white lettering, it bears the famous Joe DiMaggio quote: "I want to thank the Good Lord for Making Me a Yankee." I can't tell you what he paid for it, but Derek got the sign.

While we were digging around the stadium, we found a duplicate Thank the Good Lord sign hanging outside the press room. We put that one up for auction, and in the end, Hideki Matsui won it. He hung it up in the Hideki Matsui Baseball Museum in Ishikawa, Japan.

THE BLACK

On October 18, 1977, the Yankees hosted the Los Angeles Dodgers for Game 6 of the World Series. The Yanks were up 3 games to 2. During batting practice, Reggie Jackson, the Yankees electrifying and polarizing right fielder, smashed 18 balls over the outfield wall.

"Save some of those for the game," second baseman, Willie Randolph, told him.

"There are more where those came from," Reggie responded.

Sure enough, Reggie went on to enjoy one of the most spectacular individual games in baseball history, mashing three consecutive home runs. The action began in the fourth inning, with the Dodgers up 3-2.

As Thurman Munson stood on first, Jackson nailed Burt Hooton on his first pitch sending the Yanks ahead with a 4-3 lead. Later in the fifth with two outs and Willie Randolph on first, Reggie launched another rocket off Elias Sosa that landed in the right-field seats. Finally, he electrified the home team crowd of 56,407 by leading off the eighth with the historic blast into the center-field bleachers. Mr. October indeed. Riding on the five runs batted in (RBIs) of their slugging champion, the Yanks showed a glimpse of what Yankee baseball was and held on for the 8-4 victory that earned their twenty-first World Series title. It was the first crown for the Bronx Bombers since 1962.[1]

Reggie's final blast was a 475-foot moon shot to dead center. The ball landed in The Black of Yankee Stadium. This was the famous empty section of the bleachers behind the center-field wall, painted black to protect the batter's sightline, and forever off-limits to fans. Only the most mammoth homers reached The Black, whereupon the little white ball would ricochet around that giant space like a pinball. Only a handful of sluggers reached The Black in any given season, and no one reached it as many times as Reggie. Because of this, he was called the Mayor of the Black.

---

[1] From *The Baseball Almanac* http://www.baseballalmanac.com/ws/yr1977ws.shtml

We weren't planning to remove The Black, but one day we got a call from the mayor.

"What are you doing with The Black?" Reggie said. "I want to partner with you on that black. I did a photo shoot out there, and I think it was a key part of my career."

That call was all we needed. We knew what we had to do. We cut out square-inch swatches of The Black, and framed each one with an autographed photo of Reggie, and a descriptive plate. They've sold surprisingly well.

Reggie also bought the giant blue metal and Lucite letters that sat atop the ballpark, identifying it as YANKEE STADIUM.

THE FOUL POLES

Johnny Damon called about a foul pole. He wanted to partner with some of his Yankee teammates to buy a foul pole, and donate it to a public park. We saved it for him for a little while—until Johnny found out that local ordinances in the California town where the park is wouldn't allow him to install something that tall.

Even I hadn't originally considered the foul pole to be something we could sell. It was so big. But in the end, I realized it was no different from the other oversized items. We cut it up into hundreds of pieces, and sold each piece in a glass case, with a descriptive plate. Turned out to be one of our best-selling items.

I have a length of the old right-field foul pole in my house.

It's the coolest coat rack I've ever seen.

THE CLUBHOUSE CARPET

About that clubhouse carpet George Steinbrenner and Roger Clemens once stood on, spraying each other with champagne?

It was too large to sell to one person, but needless to say, that didn't stop us.

We cut up the carpet and sold it as doormats and car mats.

NOTHING BUT
A DREAMER

People ask me, "What makes a successful entrepreneur?" But I think a better question is, "Who makes a successful entrepreneur?" The businesspeople I know who have risen to the top all have highly active and creative minds. They're daydreamers, and have been since they were young. The question of *What Else* has always come to them intuitively.

When I was a kid growing up in Brooklyn, I was responsible for my own entertainment most of the time. I was the kind of kid who would walk down the street and slam into a lamppost because my mind was off on some adventure. Then I'd look up at the lamppost and think, "Would you look at this thing? There's nothing on it. I bet I could make some money with it. It's an opportunity!" Because money was always scarce in our family, it was constantly on my mind. My daydreams were usually about making money.

For the most part, the way I think hasn't changed much since I was that kid. I still talk to myself all the time, still daydream. My mind is always racing: 24/7 365. And while it often takes me to some deep, dark places, I usually come out with some really weird, interesting ideas. People don't even understand what I'm saying because I've gone so far down the rabbit hole in my own head. My right-hand man, Eric Levy, likes to say I have "Idea Tourette's."

* * * * * * *

A few years ago, Mara and I took our two kids to Israel. We were going to see the whole country. We landed in Jerusalem, and our first stop was the Wailing Wall. Part of an ancient temple, the wall was built in 19 BC.

When we got there, part of it was being restored and although it was partially blocked with scaffolding and tarp, the Wailing Wall was still a really awe-inspiring sight.

We stood in front of the wall and listened to the tour guide tell us its history. It was built by King Solomon and survived occupations during the Roman Empire, the Middle Ages, and the Ottoman Empire. Jewish people make pilgrimages from all over the world to see it.

Staring at the wall, I couldn't help but start daydreaming. While everyone else was marveling at these ancient ruins, entrenched in their history, I was playing out a completely different scenario in my twisted mind.

I started making believe that somehow I got fired at Steiner. And as if I were living in a Hitchcock thriller, someone took away all my money and I had to leave the United States immediately. How would I earn a living abroad?

Standing in its long shadow, I looked up at the Wailing Wall.

"This place could be a souvenir gold mine," I thought. "I can't believe they're missing it."

I played the whole scenario out in my head.

I would move to Israel, convince the tour guide to partner up with me, and start a new business.

"We're going to start a collectibles gift shop," I'd tell him. "Right at the base of this wall."

I thought of all the different products we could create around the wall, the whole biblical site. There were thousands of years of history and meaning people could have a piece of.

By the end of our tour, I had already built an entire store in my head. And there was a line out the door. I could see it all so clearly.

We got back to the hotel, and I thought, "That was a weird daydream." But then I wondered, "Is there something there I can actually work with?"

The next morning, I called my friend Paul Packer. I had met Paul a few years prior, working on a Derek Jeter–funded program that sent disadvantaged kids to summer camp. Paul manages an equity fund in New York, and is on the Pro–Wailing Wall Committee, which promotes Jewish rites at the wall. He has some good connections over there.

I proposed we create a Wailing Wall product line, complete with paperweights and key chains filled with authentic sand and dirt from the site. Those sorts of things. Maybe we could sell some of the bricks and stones themselves. People who weren't lucky enough to see the Wailing Wall in person could at least buy a keepsake with an authentic connection to it. We could donate a healthy portion of the proceeds to the renovation. We'd give it a shot in the arm, and make a little money ourselves. Everybody wins.

We're working on this project even as I write this.

In the States, "new" Yankee Stadium is my holy land. I've been to the new building hundreds of times, but I still look at it with fresh eyes. "What's missing here? Which players are getting the biggest reactions from the fans?" I look at every aspect. "Could that billboard be relocated? Could that banner be sold?"

I look at Mariano Rivera sitting on the bullpen bench, and I think, "Can we get that bench and sell it? Wouldn't that be cool? What about the bullpen phone? If you owned a restaurant, wouldn't it be cool to have the Yankees bullpen phone in it?"

I get in those phases, I start daydreaming, and everything looks like that lamppost I thought about when I was a kid.

FRESH EYES

Finding the little kid in myself is something I work at, too.

After my son left for college a couple of years ago, I befriended the son of my good friend and Scarsdale neighbor, Jim Ross. Jim's son Alex was around 10. I took him to ball games and athlete appearances and events whenever I could. I wanted to see the world through his eyes.

My wife used to laugh at me.

"You know," Mara would say, "that's not your son."

But that's my business. Finding the little kid in everybody. That way of looking at the world—with a sense of wonder and imagination.

When I go to a game, and a kid stops me, I always listen to what he has to say. Then I pitch him ideas. I tell him to e-mail me if he thinks of anything I can use.

We have so much to learn about all areas of life from kids. No matter how old we are or how much experience we have, we can always learn something from each other—even from the youngest of us.

Sandlot Wisdom

When I was growing up in Brooklyn, I often relied on my friends' parents for words of wisdom, a place to hang out, food—all sorts of things. Due to my family's circumstances, I was a bit more wanting than my friends, but we all relied on—and got to know—various adults in the neighborhood. People made it their business to contribute to the betterment of the community, particularly the kids. That was just routine. The whole community was healthier for it.

In this way, my old neighborhood was very much on my mind when I volunteered to coach my son's Little League team. In addition to wanting to pass my own love of sports to another generation, I wanted to pay forward all of my old Brooklyn mentors. And I knew working with the kids would help me stay grounded. Helping children is spiritually nutritious.

Starting when Crosby was 11, through his final season at age 14, I coached the Scarsdale Pirates, Diamondbacks, and Devil Rays, respectively. And I think that in those three seasons, I learned more from the Little Leaguers than they learned from me.

Kids experience the same emotions adults do, and they're motivated and inspired by the same kinds of feelings that we are. But because these forces act on children in a more transparent manner—kids don't disguise their feelings the way adults do—observing them is a good way to learn about yourself and others. They're not conscious of this themselves, but the lessons kids learn on the ballfield—or where I'm from, on the sandlot—are lessons that will apply throughout their entire lives. Lessons we all could afford to be reminded of now and again.

All this is to say that coaching little leaguers to success is not so different from managing and motivating a successful team in business; it's just that the lessons are more straightforward. Whether you are coaching a team or managing a division or company, the same concepts apply.

I want to share with you a few of my coaching techniques.

GET EVERYONE TO BUY IN

The first thing I did as a coach at the open of every season was host a pizza party at our house for all the players on the team and their parents. It was a chance to introduce myself to the kids and parents, and for them to get to know each other. It was essential that all the principals involved be familiar with one another. Whether playing or coaching—or simply living with players or coaches—everyone was an important part of the team.

After introducing myself to everyone, and going over some preliminary stuff, I asked everyone a simple question:

"Do you want to play to have fun?" I asked. "Or do you want to do what it takes to win the championship?"

We'd take a vote. Play-to-win would always come out on top.

This was so important. By taking that vote, I gave them agency to help decide how the team was run. Having given them a choice, it was easier to ask them to make the sacrifices necessary to win. Ensuring that the players were on the same page as the coaches meant that when I held extra practices, kept them late, or pushed them to tap abilities they didn't know they had, they understood why I was doing it. And I got the parents to buy in, too. It was important that when the kids got home from practice, they had the support and understanding of their families as well. Without it, the next practice might not go so smoothly.

That principle applies to managing adults, as well. You have to make sure your team has crystal-clear goals in mind—goals that all members are invested in reaching. Only when everyone is on the same page, moving in the same direction, does the whole of the team become greater than the sum of its individual members.

Make Sure Individuals Know What's Expected of Them

While it's imperative to establish group goals, it's just as important to outline goals for each person. A good worker will always be invested in the success of the "team," but he will also naturally desire personal growth.

So another thing I always did at the beginning of each season was to ask the kids to write down their individual goals—which position they each wanted to play, which position they were best at, which skills they wanted to improve, and where, ultimately, they wanted to end up. I'd meet with each of them, and go over what they wrote. I'd explain to them what they'd have to do, in my eyes, to earn their desired position, and to improve in the areas in which they wanted to get better.

I'd have similar discussions with each player before every game; together, we tracked their progress throughout the season. This was another way of making them feel important and cared for. People perform at their best when they feel a high sense of self-worth.

Also before each game, I went over the starting lineup and positions, even though those things almost never changed game to game. And we reviewed the game plan before every game as well, even if that never changed.

As a coach or a manager, it's important to show that organization is a priority to you, day in and day out. An organized manager usually has an organized team.

When you're a manager, your team is a reflection of you. People like to say, "It's the players that play the game." But the players usually take on the coach's personality, and that fact comes through over the course of the season. In a similar way, an office takes on the personality of the manager or chief executive.

Coaching is not just about the x's and o's of the plays. It's about the people and relationships. In business, I say, "It's not what you know; it's what you can sell." I never played much baseball, but I was able to sell my way of playing the game because I got my kids to trust me, and to trust in themselves.

And I have to do the same thing every day with my team at Steiner.

If You Can't Motivate, Incentivize

One season, after coaching the Pirates for a few games, I noticed that the kids had trouble throwing out runners at home plate from the infield. It was a weakness that could be the difference between a win and a loss in a close game.

I started having them do a new drill in practice. In this drill, the kids stood around the infield taking turns trying to hit a garbage can I placed at home plate as a proxy catcher. But the first few times we did it, the kids found the drill boring, and they were lackadaisical.

I tried to explain how important it was to hone certain fundamental skills, like throwing home accurately, but it wasn't connecting in their heads. In Little League, having to throw a runner out at home from the infield is pretty rare. Because the skill doesn't come up a lot in games, the kids didn't feel compelled to devote themselves to learning it.

But I came up with a solution.

The next time we did the drill, and the kids' lethargy continued, I stopped it in the middle. Then I walked to my car, and I came back to the field with a box of Pokemon trading cards and 10 signed baseballs. I always have that kind of stuff lying around in my car.

"The first time you hit the garbage can, you win a pack of Pokemons," I announced to the team. "The second time, you get an autographed baseball."

Wouldn't you know it? All of a sudden, they couldn't get enough of the drill.

Every time I said, "It's getting late, we can stop practice now," the team yelled out, "No!"

The team insisted on staying long past the scheduled end of that practice.

By the time we finally left the field, the sky was dark, there wasn't a single photo left—and the garbage can looked like Swiss cheese.

Whenever possible, motivate and inspire your team to see the value in hard work or in learning something new. But when all else fails, don't be reluctant to "incentivize" (read: bribe) them. Better they learn on account of a material reward than not at all.

MAKE EVERYONE FEEL IMPORTANT

My first season coaching Little League, I had almost no idea what I was doing. It was kind of a disaster. I took it too seriously, and I don't think the kids had as much fun as they should have. I may preach not playing the score, and not to care too much about winning and losing, but whatever team we were playing back then always seemed to care just enough to beat us! We didn't win a single game.

Fortunately, many of my business associates had experience in this area. I was lucky enough to get great advice from friends like Ozzie Smith, Tony Gwynn, Dave Winfield, and Stan Musial. It amazed me how many details they all remembered from playing ball as little kids.

One thing these guys all agreed on was that the key to coaching a Little League team is to make each and every kid on the team feel important, regardless of their skill level or position. I placed a premium on this during my second season.

To convey to the team how important every player was, I opened the first practice with a story I picked up from another friend who had given me some great advice on Little League coaching, Bruce Eagle.

Bruce told me that the first championship game he ever coached ended in dramatic fashion. The kid who played left field for him, a 12-year-old named Danny, hadn't seen much action over the course of the season; balls were rarely hit to him, and as a batter, he rarely got on base. Bruce tried to engage him as much as possible during practice, always reminding him that on pickoff attempts at third, and balls hit to right field, Danny had to back up the third baseman in case of an overthrow.

Still, if Danny already lacked confidence when the season began, he really felt like he was inconsequential by the time of the title game. He didn't think he had contributed in a significant way to any of the team's wins. To make matters worse, he had a poor day at the plate, failing to reach base each time he came up to bat in that title game.

Bruce's team was leading by one run when they took the field in the bottom of the final inning. They got two quick outs, but the next kid up was the other team's best player. Sure enough, he mashed a ball to deep right, over the fielder's head. Everyone knew it was at least a double right off the bat; but the hitter had other intentions, because he rounded second base at full speed, without even looking up. At the same time, the right fielder finally ran down the ball. He fired it to his cutoff man, the second baseman. The second baseman then whipped around and threw to third, but his throw was clearly way too high; it sailed over the third baseman's head. Seeing this, the third base coach waved the runner home, expecting to tie the game.

There was only one problem there; just as he was accustomed to doing in practice, Danny had run down the left field line, to back up the third baseman. What looked like an overthrow to third ended up being a perfect throw to Danny. With the runner well on his way home, Danny caught the ball and made the throw of his life, firing a strike to the catcher, who tagged out the runner. Game over. Bruce's team had won the championship— with Danny getting the crucial final out.

"Everyone here is important to this team," I'd tell my players. "Whether they know it yet or not."

At Steiner, when we get an order for a collectible, it goes from the salesman on the phone, to the picker in the warehouse, to the guy who packages it and ships it out. And even before all that, there's someone—likely an executive—who set the price for that item when we acquired it in the first place.

Each of these employees works in a different part of the building. They all have different salaries and responsibilities—but they're all important to the process. Just because one guy is packing a box doesn't mean he's not a crucial part of the company. Everyone has to do their part, as diligently as possible; if any one person drops the ball—or forgets to cover—it screws up the whole order. Everyone is important, and they have to feel that way for the company to be successful.

CONCLUSION

WHAT MAKES YOU TICK?

My career has taken all sorts of twists and turns; I went from working in hotels to managing restaurants; from marketing events to hiring celebrity bartenders; from organizing and hosting athlete appearances to running corporate promotions and PR; from running a memorabilia company, to selling dirt, and even to overseeing the demolition of Yankee Stadium. How could I have been committed to any one of these things if I ended up going from each of them to the next?

The answer is that all along, I was committed to something very important. At each stage, I provided a particular service to people. From managing the Hard Rock, to hiring Wayne Gretzky as a bartender, to reuniting Yogi Berra with Yoo-hoo, to selling a Notre Dame jersey or a seat from Yankee Stadium, I've always been committed to delivering something valuable to people, something that provided them enjoyment in some way—a piece of history or a chance to have a piece of an idol or hero.

I asked Mara what she remembered about my attempts to court her, and she unearthed a memory from our first meetings, at Camp Sussex, when we were just 17.

"There was a Dairy Queen up the road from camp," she said. "You used to bring me ice cream late at night, when I couldn't get out. A whole pint of custard. When you saw how popular it was, you started bringing it for my whole bunk. The girls loved you."

Beyond an agent, or a salesman, or a marketer, I'm a people person and a service provider; no matter my job, I have stayed true to that quality.

"It's part of your soul," Mara says. "You don't want to see anyone else go through what you went through as a child. You've made it clear to our children that they should always be the first people to volunteer to help someone. We could see a stranger on the street who tells you, 'I love Derek Jeter,' and you'll get their address and just send them a Jeter item. You like the feeling of people saying, 'This is great. Thanks so much.' I think that makes you tick."

The business world is so much different from what it was when my generation was coming of age. The roads to success are varied, and some aren't even visible. Four out of 10 jobs in the private sector didn't exist ten years ago. Fifty percent of the companies that will make up the S & P (Standard & Poor's) in 2020 haven't yet been formed. It's impossible to predict what the next big skill to have will be, or where the next big market will be.

When my generation got out of college, there were clearer career paths laid out for us. With blue-chip companies like IBM, General Motors, Frito-Lay, and Procter & Gamble thriving, a person could aim for an entire career in one company. That was a way to plan out a life.

Accordingly, commitment and diligence are more important than ever, because those are the skills that translate to any field, to any market, no matter how the outside world changes. Automatic or not, being committed to your own beliefs and goals—to what makes you tick—is crucial to a successful career. If you stick to your core beliefs, you'll be prepared when the next big opportunity presents itself. If you don't, you'll just be chasing opportunities that other people will be better equipped to capitalize on.

Take the woman I spoke to at my synagogue—the one who left her job in book publishing to go into the real estate business, only to find that it wasn't so welcoming. I wonder if, when making the change, she stayed committed to her core.

As a book publisher, she was certainly a service provider—something she'd be as a real estate agent. But book publishing is also based on providing and creating content, as well as working with a steady group of people from project to project. A real estate agency focuses on selling things—properties—that other companies create, and requires doing business with different people virtually every day. It would take someone years to catch up on the necessary skills that go into that manner of doing business. It's too big a jump to hit the ground running.

You can't possibly invest all your energies in something that doesn't move you personally. So you need to invest in the type of career that resonates in your heart, even more than in your head.

You have to have the confidence to stick to that path. To be true to your core passion and knowledge, and to let them propel you through your career—and help you adapt to all the changes along the way. You gotta have the balls to play the long game.

Not the score.

STEINERISMS

Ever since JJ told me his "truths" in Baltimore some 30 years ago, I've been a big collector of maxims focused on life and work. Sure, these kinds of sayings sometimes come off as trite, but every so often you come across one that really resonates with you. And when you repeat one of those to yourself, it can be a great guide through a particular problem, or project, or just *life*. Here are some of my favorite phrases or, as I like to call them, Steinerisms:

1. A big part of who you are is who raised you and where you grew up.
2. Do as much as you can for as many people as you can as often as you can without expecting anything in return.
3. What else × what's next = first to market.
4. Commitment is not always convenient
5. Judgment day doesn't come at a convenient time. Be your best every day, so no matter when it comes, you'll be ready.
6. My mother always said: "It's our job to do the right thing and to help others. Give to give. Don't give to judge."
7. Relationships are a mirror! If you are unhappy with your wife she is probably unhappy with you. Same goes for employees.
8. All communication is not equal.
9. In negotiating, a big part of getting what you want is helping other people getting what they need.
10. Thinking you want to be happy is not as important as understanding you deserve to be happy.
11. Your true value is determined by how much you give in value, rather than how much you take in payment.
12. Don't let a bump in the road put you on the side of the road, in a ditch.

13. The first 90 seconds minutes of your day determine the rest the other 23 hours and 57.5 minutes of your day.

14. Don't regret where you've been if you like where you are.

15. The end only justifies the means if good people don't get hurt along the way.

16. Nothing significant gets done between 9 a.m. and 5 p.m., but the things that get done then allow you to do the serious things after the workday is done.

17. The only thing you should expect from money is a better hotel room.

18. Rome wasn't built in a day, but I'm sure they were working every day to build it.

19. Vision without action is hallucination.

20. Hope is not a plan.

21. It's okay to lose, as long as you don't lose the lesson.

22. Dig the well before you're thirsty.

23. Are you spending your time, or investing your time?

24. Don't eat a hot dog—or any food—during the before the end of the first quarter or third inning of a game.

25. Don't eat sushi on a Sunday.

26. You can't outwork bad nutrition.

27. If you have more than three priorities then you have zero priorities.

28. It's risky not to take risks.

29. Just because you're a character doesn't mean you have character.

30. You can learn on the job, but that's no replacement for studying. If you want to be a great manager, read lots of

books about managing. If you want to be a great salesperson, study up on that.

31. Your best days are not your yesterdays.

32. Never meet someone, or schedule any meeting, on a Monday morning or before lunch; no one's head is in the right place at those times.

33. If you use your head, you don't have to use your feet.

INDEX

BRANDON STEINER

Photo courtesy of Toshi Tasaki.

**Have Brandon Speak at Your Next Event! Visit
BrandonSteiner.com or Call 1-800-759-SCORE**

Sports Marketing Expert

Author. Brandon is also the author of *The Business Playbook*. Released in 2003, the *Playbook* quickly became a staple in sports management and entrepreneurship classes in universities nationwide. Its lessons help students and businesspeople alike take their game to the next level.

Speaker. Brandon gives seminars, keynote addresses, and speeches directed at improving management styles and customer relations by sharing personal lessons and business techniques that helped him find success. He visits universities, organizations, corporations, and professional sports teams to give presentations that help drive sales and run businesses more efficiently.

CEO. Brandon is the founder and CEO of Steiner Sports Marketing. Founded in 1987, Steiner Sports initially started as a way to pair athletes with corporations for promotions. Since then, it has transformed into the industry leader for sports memorabilia and has sold over 20 million autographs. Today Steiner has exclusive partnerships with teams like Notre Dame and the Yankees, and with dozens of players like Derek Jeter, Hank Aaron, and Peyton Manning. *SteinerSports.com* allows fans to buy a piece of their favorite team's history with the guarantee that every item is unique, high quality, and most important—authentic.

On the Internet. Brandon's new site, *BrandonSteiner.com*, gets countless hits every day from readers and fans who want to learn more about business. It shares priceless insights into what it takes to make it in the sports world. The "Ask Brandon" section lets readers directly correspond with Brandon, who answers any questions that they might have.

Get Connected:

 Facebook.com/steiner

 @BrandonSteiner

 Linkedin.com/in/BrandonSteiner

 http://brandonsteinerblog.tumblr.com/